Cabinetmaking Procedures
for the Small Shop

by Kevin Fristad and John Ward

Cabinetmaking Procedures
for the Small Shop

Commercial Techniques that Really Work

By Kevin Fristad and John Ward

Illustrations by Gina Roman

CAMBIUM PRESS

BETHEL

ISBN: 1-892836-11-4

First printing: June 2001
Printed in the United States of America

Published by
  Cambium Press
  PO Box 909
  Bethel, CT 06801 USA
  Tel 203-426-6481   Fax 203-778-2785
  www.cambiumbooks.com
  Cambium Press is a division of Cambium Associates, Inc.

Your safety is your responsibility. Neither the author nor the publisher assumes any responsibility for any injuries suffered or for damages or other losses incurred that may result from material presented in this publication.

Library of Congress Cataloging-in-Publication Data

     Fristad, Kevin, 1949-
          Cabinetmaking procedures for the small shop: commercial techniques that really work
          / by Kevin Fristad and John Ward.
               p. cm.
          ISBN 1-892836-11-4
             1. Cabinetwork. I. Ward, John, 1944- II. Title.

     TT197 .F78 2000
     684.1'6--dc21

Table of Contents

ACKNOWLEDGMENTS

I am especially indebted to the John O'Connell School of Technology, where first I learned the art of cabinetmaking; to Jim Keith, who provided me with my initial opportunity to work in the trade; to Christopher Bratt, who instilled in me a sense of pride and professionalism; to John Petricka, who showed me that woodworking can be fun; to John Ward, for teaching me the importance of design; to Lynn Wellman and Les Asplund, for their trust and confidence; and to the countless other woodworkers I've known along the way who've shared their skill and knowledge.

To my wife, Terri, and my daughter, Willa, who have endured my many hours away at work, and who have been a genuine source of personal inspiration over the years, I dedicate this effort.

—Kevin Fristad, Fall 2000

ABOUT THE AUTHORS

Kevin Fristad works as Production Manager at a commercial cabinet and fixture company on Whidbey Island in Washington's Puget Sound. His cabinetmaking procedures have provided the form and substance of this book. Fristad first studied cabinetmaking during the 1970s at the John O'Connell School of Technology in San Francisco, CA, and has been involved in the woodworking industry ever since. Kevin Fristad and John Ward were co-workers for 11 years at Artisan Woodworkers, a design and woodworking shop located in Sonoma, CA.

John Ward, a former woodworker, designer, and entrepreneur, now facilitates the design of corporate business strategies.

AUTHORS' PREFACE

There are many talented woodworkers who have more than enough knowledge, tools, and experience to make fine household cabinets. But often when such a woodworker tries his or her hand at the craft, the end result is disappointment. There must be a better way, these woodworkers think—one that is simpler and more economical, and that doesn't sacrifice quality. What are the missing ingredients that prevent these cabinetmakers from achieving success? Typically, they are procedural horse sense and the tricks that come from long commercial experience.

This book offers methods gleaned from years in the cabinetmaking field, as well as those techniques that emphasize craft, expediency, and design. One method that we emphasize is the idea of full-scale layout; that is, developing a list of parts from full-sized key components. It's similar to the old "rod layout" system that you may have heard old guys talk about, but the difference is that you're making your marks on the cabinet parts themselves. This saves time and offers a great deal more reliability.

The techniques described in this book have been used to build cabinets that have been installed in some of the finest homes in the country. But even though the procedures can be complex, the woodwork is fairly simple and can be mastered with practice. With this book in hand, you will be able to build cabinets for yourself and others. The methods work for one cabinet, for a complete set of household cabinets, or, for that matter, multiple sets of cabinets for tract homes.

The concept of cabinetmaking is simple—to build serviceable storage boxes that fit comfortably into everyday life. These boxes inevitably have shelves, doors, and drawers. Most of them are built into kitchens and bathrooms, never to move again. The practice of cabinetmaking is another matter. A simple bath vanity contains a multitude of parts, each of which meets up with at least two others. It is essential that every part be listed, cut, and joined accurately. Then the doors, drawers, roll-outs, etc. (subassemblies that will be moved thousands of times), are fitted into their proper slots and openings.

Even tolerant consumers will balk at cheap materials, rough edges, racked frames, warped doors, and drawers that bind or fall apart. Little do they know how much care and fitting is required in the shop to produce superior results. One of the most important virtues a cabinetmaker can possess is attention to detail. A commercial cabinetmaker must add to that a sense of pace that is both satisfying and profitable.

It is our hope that woodworkers will be able to benefit from the information offered here. This manual is condensed and it is specific, so you must know at the outset that you will have to adapt our ideas to suit your particular circumstances. If you're just beginning, once you're familiar with the details of the book, the best thing you can do is make a simple cabinet. Evaluate the procedures as they actually work in your shop. Make the necessary changes, and build a few more cabinets. Along with the basic information in this book, experience and re-evaluation are undeniably the best teachers.

—*Kevin Fristad and John Ward*

INTRODUCTION

FACE-FRAME VS. FRAMELESS CABINETS

There are two fundamentally different types of cabinet construction: face frame and frameless, which is also often called European-style construction. It's important to understand the differences between the two types of cabinets, and to decide if you want to specialize in just one style. Each requires somewhat different tooling, techniques, and considerations.

Most people are probably more familiar with face-frame cabinets. In this type of construction, a frame attaches to the front of the cabinet. Hinges can be fully concealed, semi-concealed, or mounted on the surface. Frameless cabinets, as the name implies, lack a face frame. The doors are hung directly from the cabinet sides on special concealed hinges.

Does either cabinet style have inherent advantages or disadvantages? In face-frame cabinets, the face frame naturally produces a significant gap between the doors and drawer fronts, which can make construction easier in some respects since the alignment of the fronts is not as important. The disadvantage of the face-frame method is that you're buying a lot of lumber to make the face frame and then spending a fair amount of time to build, detail, and install the frame. Frameless construction requires a little more precision in cutting, since sizing and accuracy are critical. In effect, you end up with a 1/8-inch gap between your fronts, and any parts that are not square and true make this consistency difficult to achieve. The saving grace here is that the European hinges used with frameless cabinets are fully adjustable and can compensate for a certain degree of irregularity, but precision should always be a natural part of your way of working. One of the advantages of frameless cabinetry is that more interior space is available, particularly in drawers, since only the partitions separate the bays. The face frame isn't there taking up valuable space.

If you decide that frameless is the way for you to go, be prepared to educate your customers as to the advantages of this system. Many folks think that the European style consists of slick-looking plastic laminate cabinets and can't imagine them fitting in with their traditional décor. The reality is that you can build very traditional-looking cabinets using the frameless system. Any style of door and drawer front can be used—the only aesthetic difference being the width of gaps between the fronts.

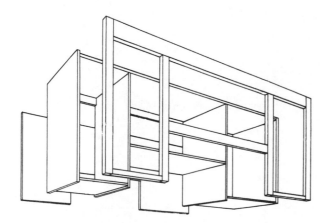

FACE-FRAME CABINETS

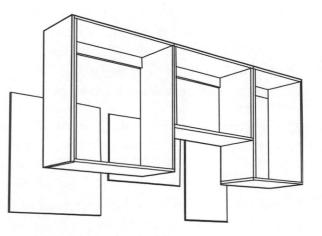

FRAMELESS CABINETS

We will cover the face-frame approach to cabinetmaking first, then talk about frameless construction in Chapter 6. You have three options for your shop—specialize in either face-frame or frameless cabinetry, or do both. There is no right or wrong way—it's a matter of personal preference. As your business grows, however, you will want to begin to upgrade or add to your machinery and equipment inventory. Since there is specialized machinery suited to both approaches, it might be wise to choose one at some point and stick with it. Also, you will be more efficient, and therefore more profitable, if you can repeat established procedures over and over again rather than switching gears each time you begin a new job. We ended up specializing in frameless cabinetry and never regretted the choice.

COMPUTERS AND CABINETMAKING

Computers are being used in most businesses today, and cabinetmaking is no exception. We have deliberately chosen to leave computer drawing, layout, and parts listing out of this discussion, and instead have focused on a basic approach that anyone can follow, regardless of computer literacy. If you're just getting started, it's important to grasp the fundamentals of cabinetmaking by doing layout manually. You can graduate to computer layout at any point, but you will have a better understanding of what's involved by doing it the old way first. If you decide that you want to use computers in the future, you'll find that there are a variety of specialized programs to choose from. Some are quite costly and, like any purchase, your workload and the size of your operation will either justify the expense or not.

We would strongly encourage you, however, to immediately start to use a computer for estimating, tracking costs, writing proposals and change orders, bookkeeping, and the other office chores that go along with making cabinets. For any business, computerization is just about essential to keep track of the myriad details that you will confront. Even if you're not currently computer literate, keep in mind that anyone can learn how to operate a computer, and in a short period of time you will likely begin to see the payoff.

TOOLING

As with the making of anything, you could probably get by with a pocket knife and a hatchet for cabinet construction if you weren't too particular about the results. Let's face it though, the more sophisticated your tools, the more leisure time you'll have at the end of the day. If every cabinetmaker were blessed with an unlimited tool budget, we'd all be in pretty good shape. But the reality is that we have to make do with what we can afford and often we can get by with very little. If you're in business to make a profit and support a family, you will need a certain level of investment in tooling, simply to maximize your efficiency. If you're a hobbyist, or on a very strict budget, or building cabinets for yourself and time is no object, you will find that you can do with very little in the way of tooling.

FINISHING

The art of finishing is a completely different and separate element of the process of cabinetmaking. We've therefore decided to forego the subject entirely, leaving this matter to the experts, which do not include ourselves.

A FEW WORDS ABOUT SAFETY

Cabinetmaking involves significant risk. We have met way too many people in the trade who have been badly injured. Almost without exception, it's because their attention lapsed for a split second. It may have been because they were too tired, too stressed out, too far behind, or just too careless. It takes only an instant for a finger or a thumb to disappear, but you're left with the effects for the rest of your life. Never remove the guards from the machinery—they're there for a reason. We also tell people that if they're uncomfortable about doing a certain procedure, they shouldn't do it. Instead they should figure out a safe approach. There's always more than one way to perform any given task.

There are other risks in the cabinet shop as well. Always wear hearing protection around all machinery—hearing loss builds up gradually and can never be reversed. Think about the music that you will want to continue to enjoy in your old age and those grandkids who will want to whisper their secrets to you in a soft voice. Use a good filter mask when working around dust. Invest in a good dust collector right from the start and hook it up to as many of your power tools as you can. Small ambient dust particles are particularly harmful. Research has shown that prolonged exposure to these fine particles can contribute to lung and/or nasal problems.

Safety glasses are essential, and you should never operate any power or pneumatic equipment without them. Even if you wear corrective lenses, it's wise to use goggles in conjunction with your regular glasses. Foreign objects can fly in from the side just as easily as they can from the front.

Back injuries are also common in the cabinetmaking industry. If you're not familiar with proper lifting procedures, visit a chiropractor, or, better yet, invite a chiropractor to your shop to give a presentation on how to lift. Also, keep plenty of waste cans around your shop so debris doesn't end up on the floor and create a tripping or slipping hazard.

Keep a well-stocked first aid kit, including an eye-wash kit, close by. Maintain it regularly to be sure that it's always ready to go if needed.

The risk of fire is always present in a cabinet shop for obvious reasons. Have several fire extinguishers on hand, and also have them inspected yearly. There are no doubt companies in your area that will provide this service. Don't even consider smoking, or allowing any of your employees to smoke, near your shop.

A good safety program contributes to your and your employees' well being, and has the added benefit of lowering worker's compensation insurance premiums. It makes good sense all around.

DON'T REMOVE GUARDS

Never remove guards from machinery. If the operation seems to require removing the guard, you're going about it the wrong way, or you're using the wrong tool.

DISCONNECT THE POWER

Before you change cutters or work inside any machine, make sure it is disconnected from electrical power. Don't rely on the on-off switch--it's all to easy too bump it on while you're working inside--and don't rely on someone else to pull the plug or flip the breaker. Be certain by doing it yourself.

CHAPTER 1: GENERAL PRINCIPLES

STANDARDIZATION

Many people resist standardization because it has the stigma of mindless production. But this is not a problem in custom cabinetry, where a variety of procedures, skills, tools, materials, and thought processes are required. Standardization of cabinet configurations and the resulting components simplifies a complex product when customers' budgets demand reasonable prices. Standardization can also mean higher profits. In this book we have specified a great number of dimensions, materials, and techniques that we accept as standard.

We are proud of our methods, but our way is only one among many possibilities. It is not important that you adopt our particular standards. It is important, however, to make choices in particular areas, standardize them for yourself, and then stick to your standards. This is not rigidity. Instead, your standards will establish a foundation to build on, and from them variations may be introduced as familiarity and skill increase. You will also find that the accuracy and discipline required to produce good cabinets will sharpen your sense of commercial pace. Using this inspiration, you will become more adept at design, making other kinds of woodwork, and making a living, too.

PRIMARY STANDARDS

The building industry deviates only rarely from the following dimensions. In a kitchen, the lower cabinet is 24 inches deep. The countertop is 25 inches deep and 36 inches from the floor. The upper cabinet is 18 inches above the countertop. It is 12 inches deep and from 30 inches to 42 inches tall. In the bathroom, sink vanities are 21 inches deep and 32 inches from countertop to floor. Appliances are manufactured to fit these standards, and you deviate from them at your peril.

SECONDARY STANDARDS

Secondary standards are a matter of choice. The drawings on the following pages show the size and material conventions we have chosen to illustrate in this book. Note that the material for the case parts can be any type of panel product from 1/2 inch to 3/4 inch thick. It's up to you. We prefer to use 3/4-inch thick utility maple or birch, or, in many cases, 3/4-inch melamine, which is a plastic-laminated particleboard panel. Thinner material will help keep the weight and cost down somewhat, but it does make it more difficult to fasten without blowing out the sides with an errant nail or screw.

UPPERS AND LOWERS OF FACE-FRAME CABINETRY

**MAIN UNITS
OF CABINET**

Ⓐ BACK
Ⓑ CASE
Ⓒ FACE FRAME
Ⓓ BASE

**COMPONENTS
OF CABINET**

① TOP RAIL
② BACK BRACE
③ STILE
④ MULLION
⑤ LIGHT RAIL
⑥ BOTTOM RAIL
⑦ TOP BRACE
⑧ TOP RAIL
⑨ STILE
⑩ MID-RAIL
⑪ MULLION
⑫ BOTTOM RAIL
⑬ FINISHED END
⑭ PARTITIONS
⑮ DECK
⑯ WALL END

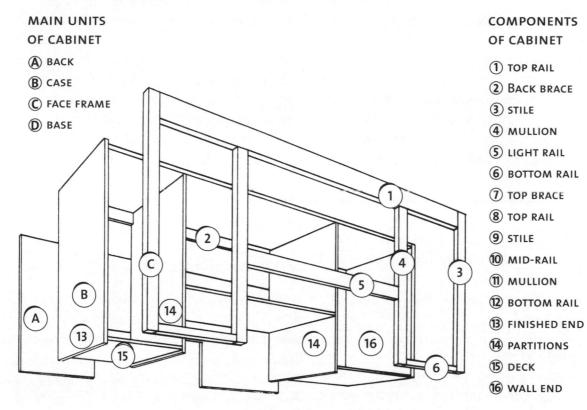

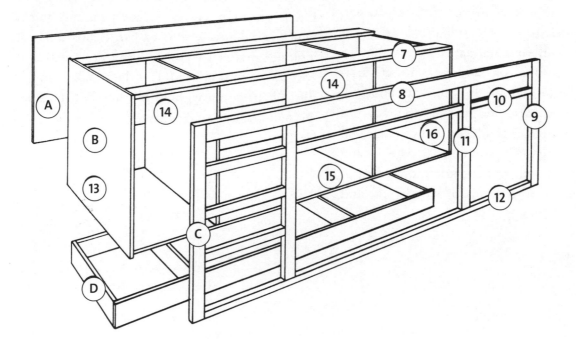

TYPICAL FACE FRAME KITCHEN CABINETS

(SUGGESTED STANDARDS ONLY: FOR PURPOSES OF DEMONSTRATION, WE USE 5/8" PANEL STOCK.)

- Ⓐ 5/8" TOP
- Ⓑ 3/4"x2" CROWN TRIM
- Ⓒ 4" TOP RAIL
- Ⓓ BACK BRACE
- Ⓔ 1/4" PLY BACK
- Ⓕ RECESSED LIGHT BEHIND 3" RAIL
- Ⓖ 5/8" ADJUSTABLE SHELF WITH SOLID EDGE
- Ⓗ 3/4" THICK DOOR
- Ⓘ 3/4" PARTITION
- Ⓙ 3/4" DECK
- Ⓚ 1-1/2" BOTTOM RAIL
- Ⓛ 3" BOTTOM NAILER
- Ⓜ MANUFACTURED TOP
- Ⓝ 2-3/4" PINE OR PLY TOP BRACE
- Ⓞ 3" TOP RAIL
- Ⓟ DRAWER BOX
- Ⓠ 3/4" DRAWER FRONT
- Ⓡ DRAWER HARDWARE
- Ⓢ 1-1/2" MIDDLE RAIL AND DRAWER RAILS
- Ⓣ HINGES
- Ⓤ 5/8" EDGE-BANDED ADJUSTABLE SHELF
- Ⓥ PARTITION
- Ⓦ 1/4" (OR 5MM, FOR FRAMELESS CONSTRUCTION) HOLE FOR ADJUSTABLE SHELF HARDWARE
- Ⓧ 1-1/4" BOTTOM RAIL
- Ⓨ 3/4" PINE OR PLY BASE

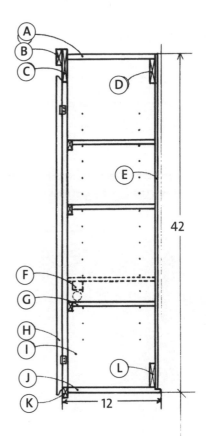

SECTION AA'

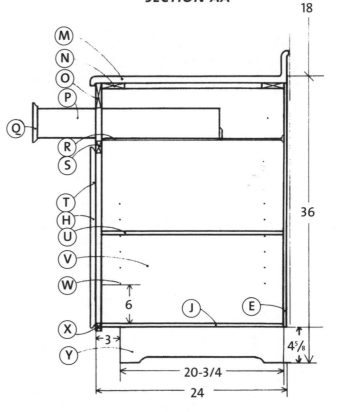

TYPICAL KITCHEN LOWERS—FACE-FRAME CONSTRUCTION

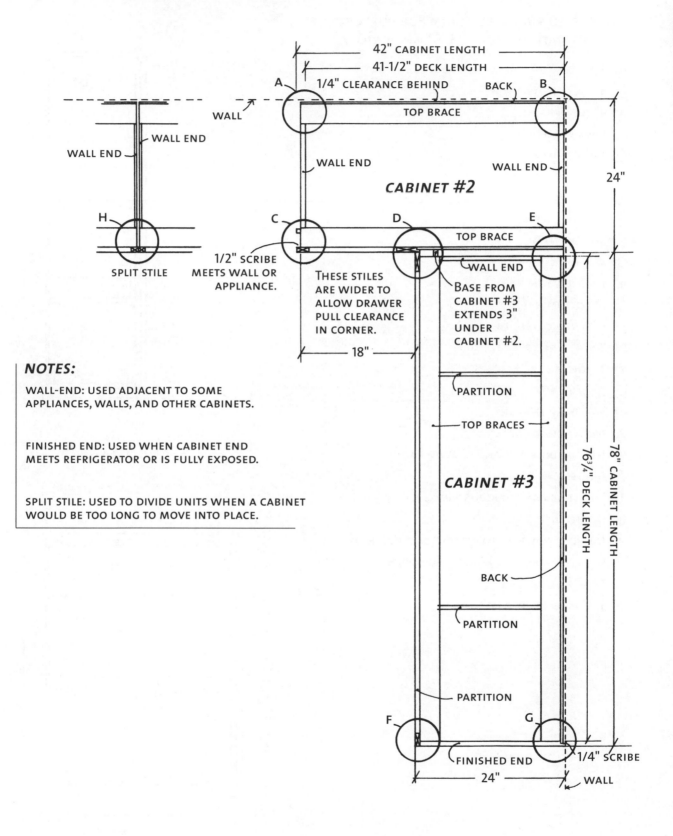

NOTES:

WALL-END: USED ADJACENT TO SOME
APPLIANCES, WALLS, AND OTHER CABINETS.

FINISHED END: USED WHEN CABINET END
MEETS REFRIGERATOR OR IS FULLY EXPOSED.

SPLIT STILE: USED TO DIVIDE UNITS WHEN A CABINET
WOULD BE TOO LONG TO MOVE INTO PLACE.

TYPICAL KITCHEN LOWERS—TOP VIEW DETAILS

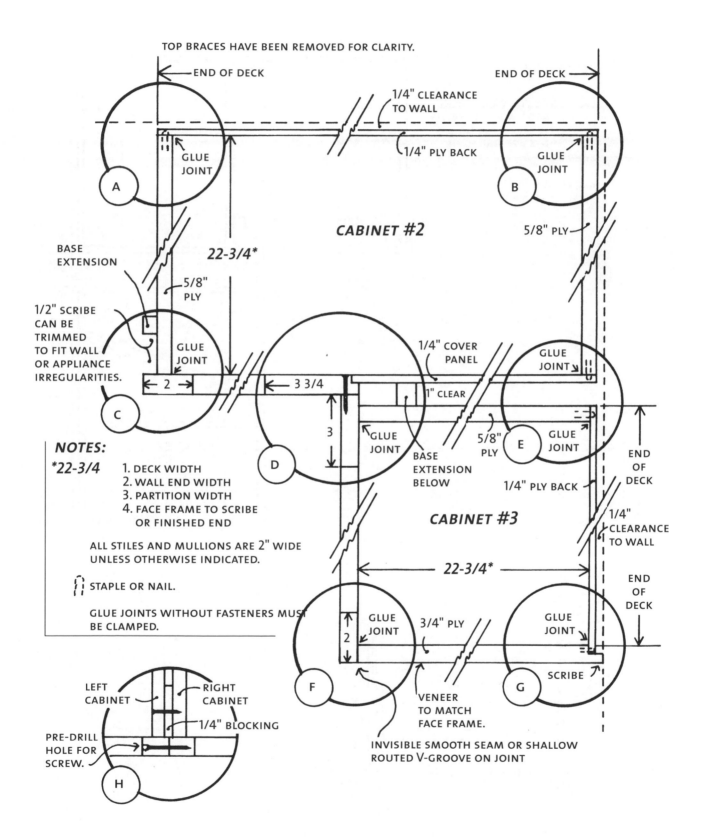

TOP BRACES HAVE BEEN REMOVED FOR CLARITY.

END OF DECK

END OF DECK

1/4" CLEARANCE TO WALL

1/4" PLY BACK

GLUE JOINT

GLUE JOINT

A

B

CABINET #2

5/8" PLY

BASE EXTENSION

22-3/4*

5/8" PLY

1/2" SCRIBE CAN BE TRIMMED TO FIT WALL OR APPLIANCE IRREGULARITIES.

GLUE JOINT

1/4" COVER PANEL

GLUE JOINT

2

3 3/4

1" CLEAR

C

3

GLUE JOINT

BASE EXTENSION BELOW

5/8" PLY

GLUE JOINT

END OF DECK

D

E

NOTES:

*22-3/4

1. DECK WIDTH
2. WALL END WIDTH
3. PARTITION WIDTH
4. FACE FRAME TO SCRIBE OR FINISHED END

ALL STILES AND MULLIONS ARE 2" WIDE UNLESS OTHERWISE INDICATED.

STAPLE OR NAIL.

GLUE JOINTS WITHOUT FASTENERS MUST BE CLAMPED.

1/4" PLY BACK

1/4" CLEARANCE TO WALL

END OF DECK

CABINET #3

22-3/4*

GLUE JOINT

3/4" PLY

GLUE JOINT

SCRIBE

2

F

G

LEFT CABINET

RIGHT CABINET

1/4" BLOCKING

PRE-DRILL HOLE FOR SCREW.

H

VENEER TO MATCH FACE FRAME.

INVISIBLE SMOOTH SEAM OR SHALLOW ROUTED V-GROOVE ON JOINT

BASES—CABINETS #2 AND #3, PAGE 29

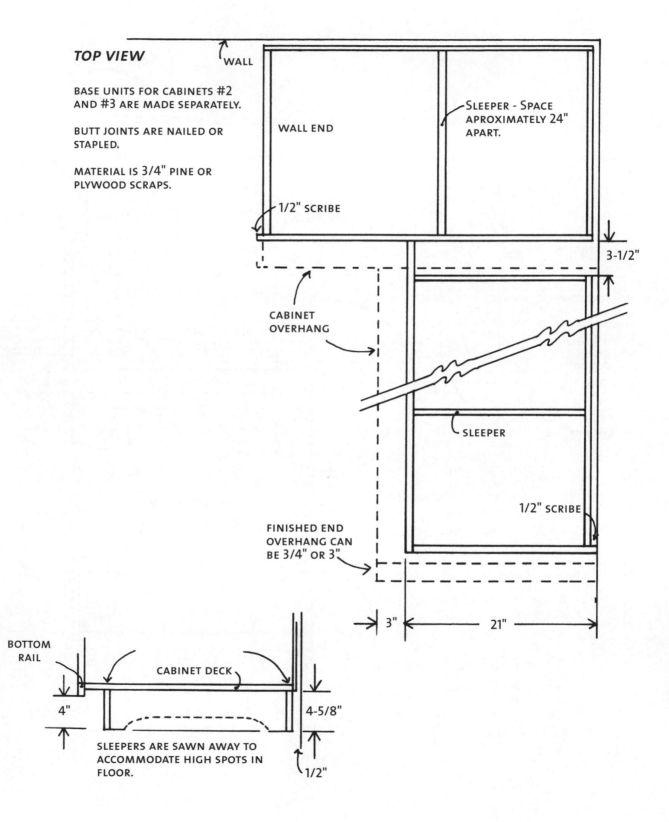

TOP VIEW

WALL

BASE UNITS FOR CABINETS #2 AND #3 ARE MADE SEPARATELY.

BUTT JOINTS ARE NAILED OR STAPLED.

MATERIAL IS 3/4" PINE OR PLYWOOD SCRAPS.

WALL END

Sleeper - Space approximately 24" apart.

1/2" SCRIBE

3-1/2"

CABINET OVERHANG

SLEEPER

1/2" SCRIBE

FINISHED END OVERHANG CAN BE 3/4" OR 3"

3"

21"

BOTTOM RAIL

CABINET DECK

4"

4-5/8"

1/2"

SLEEPERS ARE SAWN AWAY TO ACCOMMODATE HIGH SPOTS IN FLOOR.

TYPICAL CASE CONSTRUCTION

FRONT VIEWS

CASE AND FACE-FRAME RELATIONSHIP

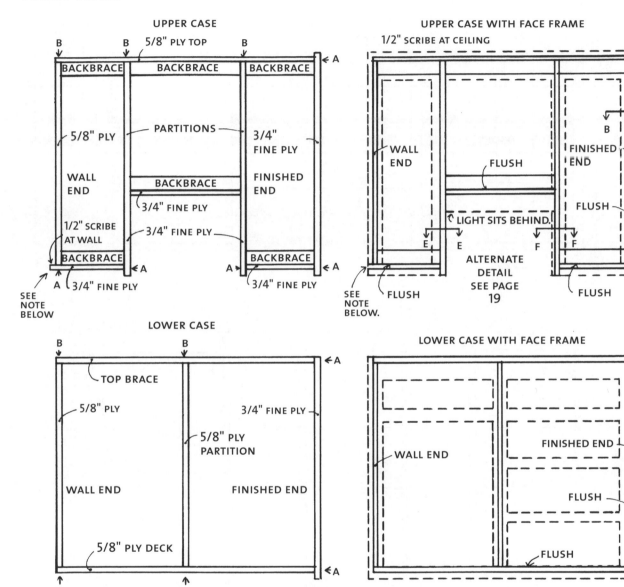

UPPER CASE
5/8" PLY TOP

B   B   B   A

BACKBRACE   BACKBRACE   BACKBRACE

5/8" PLY — PARTITIONS — 3/4" FINE PLY

WALL END — FINISHED END

BACKBRACE

1/2" SCRIBE AT WALL — 3/4" FINE PLY

3/4" FINE PLY

BACKBRACE   A   BACKBRACE   A

A — 3/4" FINE PLY — 3/4" FINE PLY

SEE NOTE BELOW

UPPER CASE WITH FACE FRAME
1/2" SCRIBE AT CEILING

B   B

WALL END — FLUSH — FINISHED END

FLUSH

LIGHT SITS BEHIND.
E E F F

ALTERNATE DETAIL SEE PAGE 19

SEE NOTE BELOW. — FLUSH — FLUSH

LOWER CASE

B   B   A

TOP BRACE

5/8" PLY — 3/4" FINE PLY

5/8" PLY PARTITION

WALL END — FINISHED END

5/8" PLY DECK

A

B   B

LOWER CASE WITH FACE FRAME

A

WALL END — FINISHED END

FLUSH

FLUSH

FASTENING CASE STRUCTURE:

A: EXPOSED SURFACE—FASTENED WITH NAILS, SET AND PUTTIED, OR SCREWS, COUNTERSUNK AND PLUGGED

B: CONCEALED SURFACE—FASTENED WITH NAILS OR STAPLED, NO GLUE NECESSARY

DOTTED LINE INDICATES FACE FRAME.

ALL SECTIONS (BB, EE, FF) ARE ILLUSTRATED ON PG. 19.

NOTE: IN UPPERS, THE DECK IS OFTEN DISCONTINUOUS. SCRIBES ARE REQUIRED AT THE WALL, ALONG THE BOTTOM, AND BESIDE RECESSED LIGHT BAYS. THE DECK MUST PROJECT INTO CORNERS TO CLOSE THE GAP BETWEEN CABINETS.

UPPER CABINET VARIATION AND DETAIL

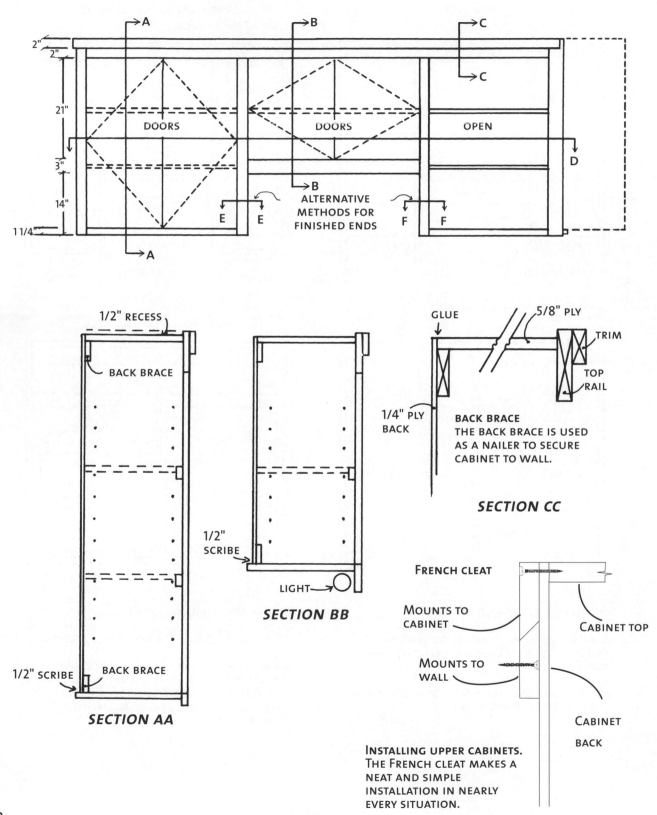

2"
2"
21"
3"
14"
1 1/4"

DOORS

DOORS

OPEN

A

B

C

C

D

E E

B

ALTERNATIVE METHODS FOR FINISHED ENDS

F F

A

1/2" RECESS

BACK BRACE

1/2" SCRIBE   BACK BRACE

SECTION AA

1/2" SCRIBE

LIGHT

SECTION BB

GLUE   5/8" PLY

TRIM

TOP RAIL

1/4" PLY BACK

BACK BRACE
THE BACK BRACE IS USED AS A NAILER TO SECURE CABINET TO WALL.

SECTION CC

FRENCH CLEAT

MOUNTS TO CABINET

MOUNTS TO WALL

CABINET TOP

CABINET BACK

INSTALLING UPPER CABINETS. THE FRENCH CLEAT MAKES A NEAT AND SIMPLE INSTALLATION IN NEARLY EVERY SITUATION.

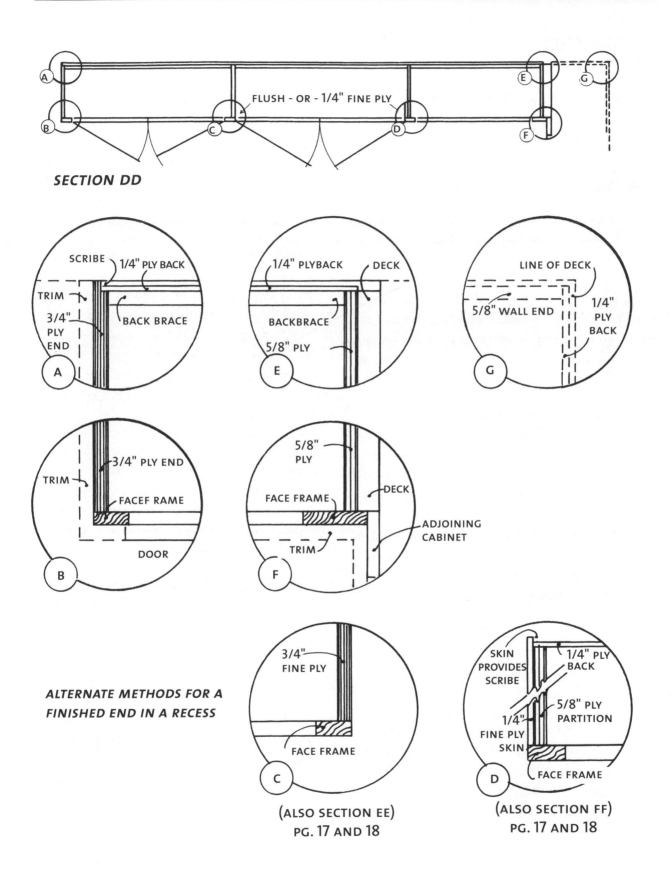

SECTION DD

FLUSH - OR - 1/4" FINE PLY

SCRIBE   1/4" PLY BACK
TRIM
3/4" PLY END
BACK BRACE
A

1/4" PLYBACK   DECK
BACKBRACE
5/8" PLY
E

LINE OF DECK
5/8" WALL END   1/4" PLY BACK
G

3/4" PLY END
TRIM
FACEF RAME
DOOR
B

5/8" PLY
FACE FRAME   DECK
TRIM   ADJOINING CABINET
F

ALTERNATE METHODS FOR A FINISHED END IN A RECESS

3/4" FINE PLY
FACE FRAME
C
(ALSO SECTION EE)
PG. 17 AND 18

SKIN PROVIDES SCRIBE   1/4" PLY BACK
1/4" FINE PLY SKIN   5/8" PLY PARTITION
FACE FRAME
D
(ALSO SECTION FF)
PG. 17 AND 18

GUIDELINES

In commercial cabinetmaking, understanding the process and knowing how to use it to economize on time and materials is of ultimate importance to staying in business.

PLANNING

Start a binder for each job of any significance (manila folders work fine for small jobs). Divide your binder into sections using tabs labeled log, drawings, contractual, materials, specifications, and any other areas you think may be helpful in organizing your material. It's really important to take a little time up front to set up a file system that works for you and to maintain this system throughout the job.

Pay attention to your clients' needs and keep them in mind at all times. It may be an overused slogan, but it's absolutely true that the "customer is always right." Be as upbeat and personable as possible during all interactions with your clients. They are spending a lot of money and need to be constantly reassured that they are getting the best. Go out of your way to communicate clearly and effectively what your clients are getting for their money.

Have a supply of contract and change-order forms made up with your letterhead or logo on them. There are a number of standard forms on the market that can be ordered with your information printed at the top. It's best to execute a signed contract for every job. This contract should spell out exactly what your client is getting and at what price. In other words, define the "scope of work." A set of scale drawings, sketches, or blueprints must be the basis of your contract and must accompany all contracts. Once again, communication is essential at this point to avoid misunderstandings later on in the job. Write up a change order for all changes that occur throughout the job, and have it signed before the changes are made. The change orders then become a part of the contract. Record any important phone calls or details in your log for future reference. You will be surprised at how often you refer back to this material.

Remember that standardization is the key to profitability. As often as is practical, try to repeat basic designs, dimensions, and procedures. Establish these standards as soon as you can and stick with them. Try to steer the customer in this direction when you're presenting your proposals. It doesn't mean that customers are getting anything less, it's simply a pragmatic approach to making a profit.

If you're thinking about borrowing money and starting a business, you should have a written business plan. There are professionals who will be able to help you with this task. In fact, a business plan will probably be required for you to obtain any funding from a lender.

Procure the best tools, materials, and shop space that you can afford. Set up an office space that's separate from the shop space. Your office activities are every bit as important as your shop activities and should be treated with the same consideration and respect.

Safety should always be the paramount consideration each time you enter the shop. A shop can be a dangerous place if it's regarded with a cavalier attitude.

PRODUCTION

Work in uninterrupted stretches of time. Have an answering machine hooked up, or, if you have someone answering your phone, have him or her take messages. Return calls at regularly scheduled shop breaks. Most of the time messages aren't urgent enough to warrant an interruption of your work.

Try to work on the entire project at once, particularly where multiple tasks are involved. You should do setups for each operation only once during the job. Plan these setups and consolidate your work accordingly.

Measure twice, cut once. No one has yet invented a reliable wood stretcher.

Material handling can be very time consuming. Try to move materials as seldom as possible, using carts or dollies wherever you can. Remember that each time you pick up a part, it costs money.

Labeling and organizing cut parts is important. It saves you from spending time later on measuring and searching through stacks to find what you're looking for.

Be purposeful. Make each step count and minimize walking around. Take the time to position your stock nearby, particularly if you're working on multiple parts. Always think ahead to the next step so you're ready to move efficiently when the time comes.

Keep your workspace clean and organized, particularly if two or more people are working together. Thoroughly clean up after each job. Dispose of leftover parts and scraps, and return tools and materials to where they belong. This process actually helps to clear one's mind and to set the tone for the next job.

Even with only three people, a shop can begin to take advantage of specialization. One experienced cabinetmaker must spend full time in the shop and be responsible for its efficient functioning. This might include all the layout, cutting, and major assembly. An apprentice would do basic subassemblies and sanding, and offer general assistance where required. You, as an owner, will be dividing your time between marketing, estimating, design, drawing, field measuring, ordering, and overall management. As your business grows, its wise to provide written job descriptions for each person in an effort to clarify roles and avoid overlap.

QUALITY

Produce the best possible cabinets for the price.

Maintain a healthy tension between perfection and commercial expediency. There's a fine line here and it's often difficult for cabinetmakers to draw that line accurately. Sometimes we find ourselves dwelling on details that only other woodworkers might notice. Put yourself in the place of your client and ask yourself if you would notice slight imperfections here or there.

While we're on the subject, clean up sloppiness all over. Reasonably careful work on cabinet underpinnings keeps you sharp for the parts that show. Consider also the importance of the client's first impression. Even parts that will ultimately be hidden should be clean and sound. If clients discover an obvious flaw right from the beginning they will continue looking and perhaps turn up other minor flaws. While these may not be important, they may contribute to a client's overall sense of uneasiness.

Lastly, but importantly, enjoy your work.

Full-size layout

The full-size layout technique we emphasize lends itself particularly well to face-frame cabinets, since these involve two elements—the case and the frame. In frameless construction, you're dealing with just one element, and it becomes about as easy to do the layout on paper, as we will see later.

When cabinet design standards have been set and specific opening widths for appliances are chosen, the only dimensions you need to begin work are the deck lengths. (See pages 30 and 31 for simplified working drawings.)

In general, when decks, ends, and partitions have been cut (see preliminary case cutting on pg. 32), actual openings and details are marked on them and the cabinet's components fall into place and are delineated. When actual sizes and configurations are seen in this manner, common sense can usually spot gross misjudgments and specific errors in measurement.

Full-size layout is one of the most important, and least known, tricks of the trade. Working this way on face-frame cabinets bypasses drawing-board speculation and brings traditional rod layout techniques right into the cabinet itself.

WORKSHOP PROCEDURE CHECKLIST

1. CUT CASES (PART 1)
Ends
Partitions
Decks
Scribe on finished ends

2. LAY OUT DECK

3. LIST COMPONENTS (PART 1)
Face frames
Shelves
Backs
Top braces
Bases
Doors and drawer fronts
Drawer boxes
Roll-outs

4. CUT CASES (PART 2)
Top braces
Back braces (uppers)
Bases
Backs
Shelves
Trim fixed shelves and cut the bands
Drill for adjustable shelves

5. STACK CASES

6. REPEAT #1 - #5 FOR UPPER CABINETS

7. CUT AND BORE FACE FRAMES

8. ASSEMBLY (PART 1)
Glue face frames
Bases
Cases
Attach face frames
Attach bases
Attach backs

9. CLEAN UP AND SAND CASES AND FACE FRAMES

10. CUT COMPONENTS
Drawers
Doors
Roll-outs
Adjustable shelves

11. ASSEMBLY (PART 2)
Drawers
Doors
Roll-outs
Accessories

12. MOUNT
Drawers
Roll-outs
Doors

13. INSPECT FOR DELIVERY

CHAPTER 2: PRELIMINARIES

CLIENT/DESIGNER/WOODWORKER RELATIONSHIPS

There are generally two markets out there—contractors who are building spec homes and homeowners themselves. If you're bidding to contractors, chances are that they will be getting several bids, and since they're in the business to make a profit, they will generally take the lowest one. It's important that you follow the plans or blueprints as a basis for your bid, and if there's a lot of vagueness, spell out exactly what it is that you are including with your proposal. Try to arrange a preliminary meeting with the contractor to review the plans and to find out what he or she is looking for. Each contractor is different. Some may want to go all out and use the cabinets as a selling point for their houses. Others may wish to feature other items and don't particularly want to spend a lot of money on the cabinets. If the contractor is building or remodeling a home for a specific client, the client will likely be in on the discussion. Sometimes contractors have a budget established for the cabinets, and they are there to assist clients in getting the best deal. Others may leave this part of the project open-ended and let clients make their own arrangements for cabinets. Since the cabinets are such a personal issue and often are one of the most expensive parts of the construction process, homeowners typically want to be involved.

Regardless of who's paying the bill, it's important to establish a personal rapport with that person in order to win trust and to make him or her feel like you will give the best possible quality and service for the money. One approach is to negotiate a price—that is, to set a rate for your time and a fair markup on materials and go from there. There is no competitive bidding.

This is an approach used more and more for higher-end woodwork and cabinetry, where there's a lot of design development and subsequent interaction between the woodworker and the client. This type of arrangement is impossible to bid anyway—it's all based on that critical element of trust.

Let's say that potential clients approach you with a vague notion of what they want for their cabinets. You sense that there's a long road ahead before a clear and coherent plan emerges. In this case, you might want to consider offering a contract for design and detailing—that is, a separate price for working with them to determine what they want, and then putting everything together into a biddable set of drawings that they will be able to take with them. At this point they would even have the option to obtain competitive pricing, since they've purchased the drawings.

Designing itself is a juggling act. People, questions, ideas, possibilities, and solutions must be allowed to interact freely for a period of time. There is no direct route to a final plan and often there is a lot of backtracking and changing of minds. This is normal. Learn to work patiently at this stage. Listen to the client's wishes about how the kitchen, for example, is supposed to feel, what specific features are wanted, and what the budget is. Almost every customer wants a new set of cabinets to be unique and there are a great many options to choose from. Choices include wood type, finish, door and drawer front styling, face frame or frameless, the type of hinges and pulls, crown molding, and a variety of other details. Other more general factors to consider are patterns created by textures, lines, lips, shadows, and arrangements of elements. Try to be sensitive to how these various details and combinations will feel to the ultimate user. You will obviously need to be well informed and confident if you're going to take on this role. Your sources might include magazines, books, home shows, interaction with other designers and woodworkers, and just about anything else that will enable you to develop an astute sense of style, design, and proportion. If you're ultimately going to be the maker of what you're designing, remember to be realistic about what can be accomplished in your shop. There are industrial techniques in the cheapest factory-made cabinets that require extensive setup, making them much too costly for a small shop to reproduce. And there are traditional design and craft skills that are far beyond the level of the average beginner. Good design comes from the cultivation of visual thinking in conjunction with common sense and immediate working capacity. It's a very individual matter.

ESTIMATING

People by nature want to be liked. One way to ensure good will, many believe, is by offering low prices for goods and services. This way of operating seems to be especially characteristic of artists and craftspeople—they tend to sell themselves short. They think: "Am I charging too much? Will clients think I'm crazy if I give them this outrageous price? Will they go somewhere else? Will they throw me out of the room after I tell them what their kitchen's going to cost?" The only way to overcome these fears is through a sensible, pragmatic approach to estimating.

So how do you go about figuring out what your products and services are worth? Let's assume that you are bidding a clear "scope of work." In other words, all the details have been worked out and the plan is down on paper. This could be in the form of architectural drawings, your own drawings, or the client's. Start with the materials. List everything that will be going into the job, right down to the small items that cost only a few cents. If you end up doing the job, this list can be used for ordering as well, and if everything is included, you've not only charged for it, you won't forget to order items later on. Establish costs on everything while maintaining

current price lists for plywood and lumber. The wood products market is a volatile one and prices can fluctuate weekly.

Next, "build the project in your head." Write down all the steps that will be necessary to do the work and list the number of hours each step might take. The further you break these steps down, the better off you'll be—it's much easier to determine how long a single task will take rather than a series of tasks. Be sure to include down time for setting up and then cleaning up at the end of the day: It's all part of the cost of doing the job. After you've totaled your hours, add a contingency factor of 15% just to be safe. This allows for human error and any number of other things that can come up during a job.

Add in time for the layout and cut-listing processes as well. Again, it's all part of making the project happen. Also, figure in loading and delivery costs at the end of the job. If you're installing the job, this, of course, will also be part of your bid.

The only thing left to do now is to figure out what your labor is worth. This is the hard part. Assign an hourly rate you're comfortable with and go for it. Keep in mind that if you are bidding competitively, you can't get greedy at this point or you won't have any work. Mark up your materials to pay for handling and processing. Finally, add on your overhead and profit, and come up with a total. You will probably have to wing it here until you have established a track record to really determine your overhead costs. A profit margin is essential if you want to grow, upgrade your equipment, build up your bank account, or do anything else you can think of to do with money.

Keeping track of your time is extremely important, and it's worth a mention here. Once you've begun the work, record your actual hours for the various procedures as you go. After you've completed the job, compare your actual hours with your estimates. This will not only tell you how much money you've earned, it will also give you a good feel for how to bid the next job. It's often difficult to take the time to do this analysis, but it's the only way you will be able to hone in on your costs and be assured of a fair profit at the end of each job.

Cabinets in the industry are often priced per running or linear foot. Take a look at what your costs are for labor and material per foot. Break them up between uppers and lowers. Come up with individual drawer costs, or any other item for that matter. Eventually, you will be able to assign dollar figures per linear foot to certain types or styles of cabinets, which will save you an enormous amount of estimating time in the future. Your estimate will be absolutely reliable, too, since it's based on historical analysis and not on hunches.

Linear-foot pricing works well for relatively routine work. However, if you get into bidding more specialized custom work, breaking out the materials and shop procedures is about the only reliable way to come up with an accurate estimate.

On a final note, if you lose a bid, always try to find out what the winning number was. This will help you determine what you did wrong. Perhaps you shouldn't bid against certain people who are continually coming in low because they're content to work for much less than you are. If this is the case, you might find out what your competition is in the beginning before you waste your time. Always be sure that you have a reasonable chance of getting the job before you bid it. Your time is important. Remember, too, that if you're getting everything you bid, chances are you're bidding too low. On the other hand, if you're losing out every time, you're going overboard and you need to figure out why. There's a happy medium in there somewhere.

PROPOSALS, CONTRACTS, AND CHANGE ORDERS

Once you have all your information compiled, you must put it into a format that you can deliver to your potential client. Two things are really important here: defining what you are going to do and for how much money. The look of your proposal is also important. If it's sloppy and includes misspelled words, your client will wonder what your cabinets will look like.

Obviously, there must be a basis for your proposal, such as a drawing or a set of plans. If there are a number of undefined items on these plans or drawings, you should spell out those items on your proposal. It doesn't hurt to be detailed, but you can definitely be hurt by being vague. Have you included sales tax, for example? Did you spell out a payment schedule? Have you listed your exclusions? Use generic forms that you've had embossed with your letterhead or make up your own. Whichever approach you use, it should be as thorough and professional as possible.

Try to arrange an appointment to present your proposal in person. This way you can review each item that's included with the client. Remember, you're a salesperson at this point, trying to close a deal, and every bit of charm and charisma you can muster up will help you to get the job. If you're meeting your potential clients for the first time, leave those pants with the holes in the knees and the wood putty all over them along with your politically incorrect T-shirt at home. First impressions are everything.

Change is inevitable during the course of a job and here again it is important to be clear about associated costs. Use a change-order form for every change, even if there's no price ramification. Send the clients a copy to sign. This forces the issue to be viewed as a legitimate change and it becomes a part of the original contract.

You will want to use common sense here and not get carried away. You can make small concessions and trades in the interest of continuity and good will, but be careful that you don't get sucked in to making a significant change at your own expense.

MEASURING THE SITE

Site measurement is one of the more important functions you will be performing. Here you will be gathering much of the critical information needed to build the cabinets, and if you're not careful, a very expensive loss of time and money could result. Begin by making up a checklist of everything you need to know. Here again, this approach is a foolproof way of not only catching everything, but catching it on your first trip so that you won't waste valuable time going back later for what you missed. The format of and information on your checklist may vary, but here are some important things to consider.

Take along a 25-foot tape measure, a mechanical pencil (don't use a pen), a notebook or pad of paper, a camera, and the plans or sketches. Determine the size of the room or rooms, remembering that there are always three dimensions to think about—length, width, and height. Locate all existing features such as doors, windows, plumbing pipes, and electrical outlets. It's a good idea to sketch an elevation of the wall or walls and precisely plot these items on your sketches. It's a drag to find that upon installation a water pipe or outlet falls directly behind one of your cabinet partitions. Locate where the fixtures and appliances will go. When taking measurements of existing appliances or windows, work from the nearest wall to the centerline. Mark this dimension on the plan, as well as the width of the window or sink, or the distance to the nearest wall. This gives you a double check, as shown on pages 28 and 29. Pick up cut sheets or model numbers for all the sinks and appliances or arrange to have them sent to you right away.

Sometimes there's information besides overall sizes on these brochures that may be important.

Take pictures of unusual situations for later reference. This is particularly useful if you will be trying to explain an odd site condition to one of your employees. It's always fun to have before and after pictures anyway. Grab a photo of your client, or the contractor too for that matter while you're at it!

Note the floor material. If 3/4-inch flooring will be used, be sure to add this amount to the height of your toe kick. If you don't, your cabinets will be 3/4 inch short, but worst of all, under-counter appliances will no longer fit. If you're measuring before drywall or other wall coverings, don't forget to deduct the thickness of the material from your overall dimensions. It's a good idea to subtract this amount right on the spot so you don't forget to do it later.

Consider access to the room. Will the units fit up the stairs, through doorways, and around corners? It seems that every cabinetmaker at least once in his or her life forgets this obvious detail. It can be quite disconcerting to arrive on the site with a finished set of cabinets and find that one piece won't make it through the door. Also check to see if tall cabinets will stand up in the room without scraping the ceiling.

Finally, note access to the house itself. Can you back up close with your truck when it comes time to deliver or will you have to go around back through the shrubs? Are there mad dogs around that may try to take your leg off when you show up?

Much of this seems simple, but it's all worth doing. When you think you're all done measuring, stand around a bit by yourself and muse on the scene, particularly if you've been with others who have been talking the whole time. Review your checklist and notes and imagine the project coming together. It's time well spent.

SCHEMATIC PLANNING

Take a look at our example of a simple kitchen as shown here. Let's say the general plan has been formulated and all you need to do is make things fit. Draw the plan and elevation views of the room to scale using graph paper. Use paper that is divided up into 1/8-inch squares. It's more accurate than using 1/4-inch grids. Place the appliances first, and then plug in all the dimensions as shown. (For purposes of this manual, we have made two sets of drawings, whereas it would not always be necessary for you to do so.) Architectural plans, or plans from homeowners for that matter, are generally not specific enough for you to build directly from them. In each job, things have to be tailored exactly to the existing site conditions and here's where your site measurements come in. Draw in the cabinets and figure out what their overall sizes need to be using your room dimensions, centerlines, and allowances for appliances. At this time, it is not necessary to figure out exact dimensions with regard to door and drawer openings. This is because the layout and cutting of actual material generates all internal dimensions as the work progresses (see full-sized layout on p. 34.) This applies to both upper and lower cabinets. Note here that the standardization of components and design make this convenience possible.

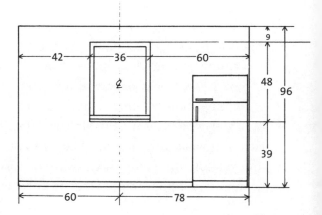

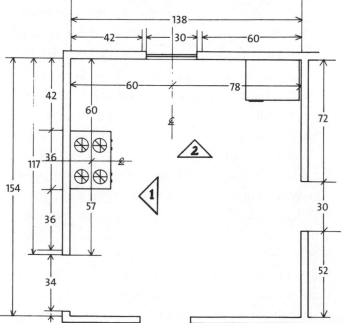

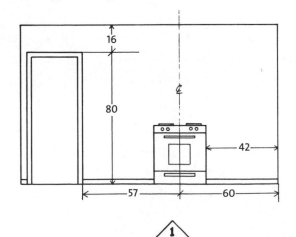

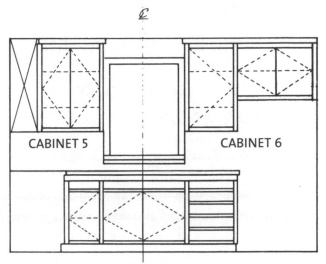

CABINET 5   CABINET 6

CABINET 3

2

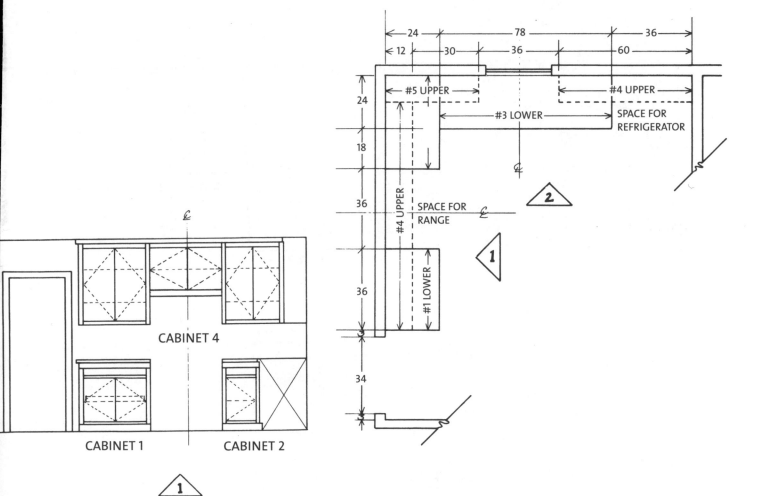

CABINET 4

CABINET 1   CABINET 2

1

CHAPTER 3

WORKSHOP PROCEDURES

DIVIDING THE PLAN INTO BUILDABLE UNITS

You've established the overall lengths of your cabinets. Once again, consider access, lifting capacity, and room size. The obvious places to divide the plan into buildable units are at walls, ends, corners, and either side of major appliances. In our example, each unit is manageable. Had one of the units ended up too long, we would have followed the procedure in Appendix 6 (page 84), pertaining to the split stile.

SIMPLIFIED WORKING DRAWINGS

Make simplified working drawings of each cabinet. These should include no more information than is absolutely necessary, as it will only add confusion at this point.

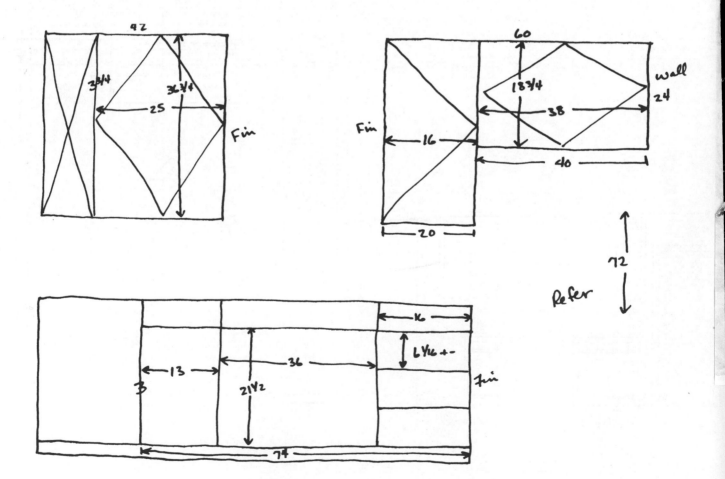

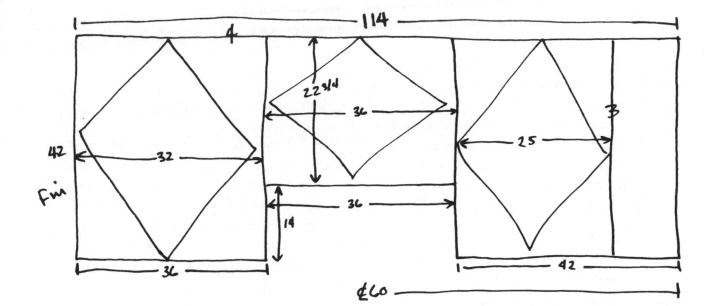

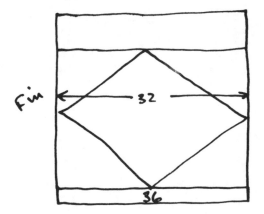

Stove

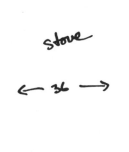

← 36 →

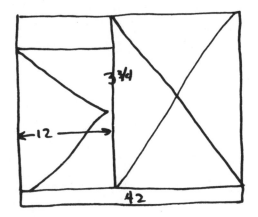

CASE CUTTING (PART 1)

The first phase of the cutting process involves those parts that will subsequently be used to generate a list of the parts for phase two. Here we'll talk about cutting lower cabinet ends, partitions, fixed shelves, and decks.

Because the cases for an entire set of cabinets will be cut at one time, the order in which you proceed can save hours of time and confusion. Whenever practical, consolidate operations and make all of the cuts for a dimension held in common throughout the job at one saw setting. This prevents variation in sizes, as it can be difficult to reset the saw exactly once it has been changed. It also ensures the uniform and tight assembly of every cabinet. Simplified operations like this make it easier to keep order in the shop. Therefore, it is very important to follow this procedure carefully.

Start out by cutting the plywood (or whatever other panel product you choose), for the cases. Note that melamine products are available with one melamine face and one wood-veneered face. If you're using flat veneered panels for the finished ends, as opposed to frames and panels, cut them first. Count up the number that you will need for the entire set and select enough material to complete this part of the work. Cross-cut the stock for the finished ends to a height of 31-1/4 inches. Then rip the material to a width of 23-1/4 inches, which will remove any chipped veneer that might have resulted from cross-cutting. Try not to use a factory edge for the front edge of a finished end—many times it is not as sharp as needed to produce a nice tight joint when the face frame is attached. Stack the finished ends in a convenient place.

Now cut the decks, partitions, wall ends, and fixed shelves to a width of 22-3/4 inches. Count up the total footage for these pieces and rip enough plywood for them. With the saw still at the same setting, cut the scribe on the inside of the finished ends. This scribe lines up directly with the back edges of all the decks, partitions, and wall ends.

CUTTING THE SCRIBE

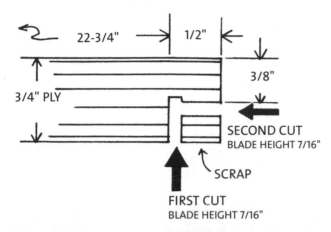

Make the first cut on the scribe with the saw blade lowered to 7/16 inch. Then reset the saw fence and make the second cut, as shown. The overshot on the first cut is intentional. It provides a clean corner for the back and a place for extra glue to squeeze out harmlessly. But if the second cut is overshot, the gluing surface will be reduced by one-third.

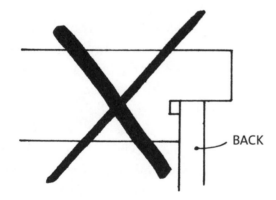

OVERSHOT ON SECOND CUT SIGNIFICANTLY REDUCES GLUING SURFACE.

Determine the deck lengths from the overall dimensions of your plan. Take into account the various details that will affect the length of the deck in relationship to the overall cabinet dimension. For example, note the 3/4 inch for the finished end and the 1/2-inch scribe needed at walls or appliances.

Cut all the decks to length from the 22-3/4-inch stock. To minimize waste, begin with the longest deck and proceed to the shortest. Next, cut your wall ends and partitions, all of which measure 29-1/4 inches long. Then cut the various fixed shelves to length.

After these lower cabinet parts have been cut, the process should be repeated for the upper cabinets. Determine the overall dimensions of your initial parts just as you did for the lower cabinets. It may be helpful to refer to the drawings on pages 17 - 19 for information on how to handle uppers with discontinuous bottoms. Upper cabinet bottoms are often made from the same finished veneered material as your finished ends, since they are exposed. These parts are 11-1/4 inches wide, as are the finished ends. Cabinet tops, wall ends, and partitions are 10-3/4 inches wide.

Having cut these parts, proceed to the full-sized layout of each cabinet's remaining parts.

FULL-SIZED LAYOUT

In layout, the size of nearly every part of an entire set of cabinets can be established with confidence and little chance of error. Marking the details on key horizontal and vertical members of the cabinet—the deck and a finished end or wall end—is the heart of the procedure. Cabinetmaking involves so many interdependent parts that you'll really appreciate the accuracy of this method once assembly begins.

An upper cabinet whose bottom deck is interrupted by a range hood or because of a recess above a sink, for example, is of little use in laying out dimensions. In this case, the layout should be done on the top of the cabinet, which is continuous.

By measuring and marking directly on the pieces that have just been cut—the decks, finished ends, and wall ends—the sizes of countless cabinet parts can be determined by direct measurement. As each detail is marked, it leads to the next one.

When laying out cabinet pieces by marking the sizes and locations on the decks and ends, you should also be compiling cutting lists of parts. By the time the lists are complete, the dimensions of the parts of the face frame and the locations and sizes of the partitions, wall ends, finished ends, shelves, shelf edge bands, roll-outs, drawer fronts, drawer box parts, and doors will all be established. You will have, in hand, reliable cutting lists for all the components and will be able to proceed to the next stage with relative peace of mind. There is little need to prefigure internal dimensions ahead of time if the standards outlined here are adopted. Hours at the drawing board are thus eliminated, as measurements are taken directly from the deck and the ends. In addition to being more efficient, this system also reduces errors and inconsistencies.

To begin layout, take a simplified working drawing and place one of the freshly cut longer decks at a convenient height in front of you. Make tick-marks at the locations of the face-frame stiles at the ends of the deck, allowing for the 1/2-inch scribe, or 3/4 inch for a finished end. See the drawing below.

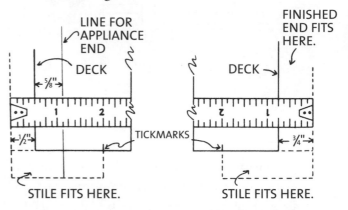

Referring to the plan, divide up the space between the end tick-marks into bays of appropriate sizes, and mark the deck for face-frame mullions at the bay divisions. If you have not already established general bay sizes, you will be doing so here. A rule of thumb is to not exceed 30 inches for an opening. Any width greater than 30 inches increases the likelihood of a sagging shelf. You should also take into account what the overall appearance will be, if you have not done so already. If the cabinet has fixed shelves, position the previously cut shelves in their proper locations and draw a fine pencil line on the deck directly along each end of each shelf. This line locates your partition. You might take a scrap of your case material and use it as a spacer as you draw your lines. Sometimes panel products vary slightly in thickness. This ensures an exact fit during assembly.

Now that the opening sizes have been delineated, mark the openings on your plan, if you have not already done so during your initial overall sizing. If you have already figured out what the openings will be on paper (in simple cabinets, this is easy to do), this step is an actual full-scale verification of your accuracy. You'll use these opening sizes later on to determine face-frame configurations and the size of your doors, drawers, and rollouts. During cutting and layout, lightly label the parts at hand to reduce confusion and increase your pace during assembly. You might experiment with various labeling systems until you come up with one that works for you. Try to label your parts in places that will not show after the cabinet is assembled in order to avoid having to go back and sand off the markings once the cabinet is assembled. These labels should be easily viewed, however, after the parts are stacked.

In the same manner, take an end or partition and mark the heights of door and drawer openings on the front edge. If there are several different configurations for the various bays, make your marks on the adjacent partition or end as well. Again, after making your marks, write the opening dimensions on your plan the same as

you did for the width of the openings. Also be sure that you have made a line 1-1/4 inch up from the bottom of any finished end, because the deck butts up to the finished end just below this line. With a carpenter's square, draw lines to indicate the location of partitions and ends on the deck, as shown.

UPPER CABINET LAYOUT

As mentioned earlier, the layout for upper cabinets with a discontinuous lower deck will need to be done on the top deck of the cabinet. Lay out your lines just as you did for the lowers. Since you're using the cabinet top instead of the lower deck, you will need to be careful not to get the face frame reversed. To avoid this, lay out your marks on the edge away from you, rather than the edge facing you. On upper cabinets with continuous lower decks, go ahead and lay out your marks in the conventional way.

MARKING PARTITIONS AND ENDS

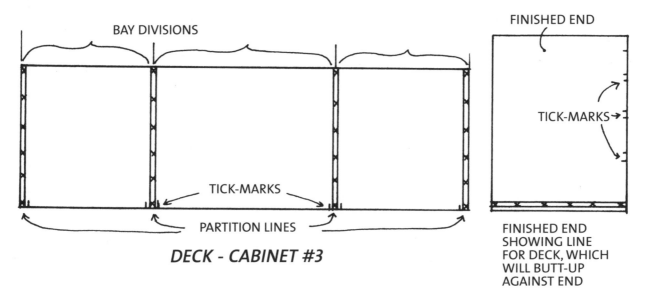

DECK - CABINET #3

LISTING COMPONENTS

Now that the key horizontal and vertical members have been marked, you can list the various components. As mentioned earlier, the cut lists that you will now be compiling will include almost all of the remaining parts for your cabinets. Regarding doors, drawer fronts, and rollouts (if any), however, we will only be listing their overall sizes at this point. In a later chapter, we will be discussing the various components of these items more extensively. You will, however, need to know which door and drawer-front style you will be using (see page 38) to come up with your overall sizes. Incidentally, when noting sizes, it's standard practice to write the thickness dimension first (if applicable), the width next, and the length or height last.

Work with the aid of the shop drawings, a deck, an end, and a large pad of paper. There should be a dedicated column for each component (one for face frames, for example, another for shelves). Tally up all the parts of the cabinet at one time. Then go to the next cabinet. These lists will include face-frame parts, shelves and bands, backs, top braces, bases, drawer fronts, drawer boxes, rollouts, and doors. When listed systematically, cutting for all similar elements for the entire job can be done at one time.

LIST THE PARTS OF THE FACE FRAME

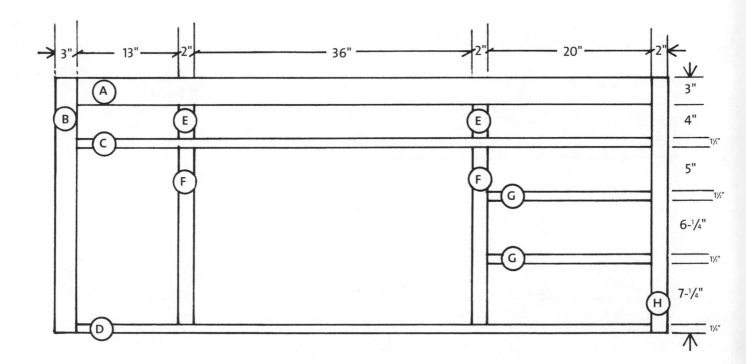

LIST ALL FACE-FRAME PARTS

When listing the top rail (a), middle rail (c), and bottom rail (d), the length is determined by the measurement between the two outside tick-marks on the deck. Dimensions for other face-frame parts are taken from the opening sizes you have just written on the plan.

LIST SHELVES

To determine the size of the shelves, measure between the partition lines on the deck. If the shelves are adjustable, subtract clearance for shelf supports, if any is required. This will depend upon the type of support you are using. If no clearance is required for the hardware itself, 1/16 inch should still be subtracted to allow for free movement up or down during adjustment. If the shelves are fixed, as they often are for lower cabinets, they will have been cut earlier with the case parts and used to locate your partitions. These previously cut shelves (22-3/4 inches deep) will need to be ripped down by the thickness of the edge-banding you plan to use for the raw front edge. After applying your edge-banding (usually 1/4 inch), these shelves will then net out at the same width as all your other case parts and will fit snugly in between the back and face frame.

LIST BACKS

Backs are cut from 1/4-inch material. The length of the back is the same as the length of the deck unless there is a finished end, in which case the back is 3/8 inch longer than the deck. This additional 3/8 inch, of course, falls into the rabbet that was cut into the finished end. The height of the backs for lowers is standard (30-5/8 inches for kitchen cabinets, 26-5/8 inches for bath vanities). The height for uppers must be taken from the layout on the vertical case parts.

LIST TOP BRACES

These are cut from 3/4-inch #3 pine or 3/4-inch plywood scrap, 2-3/4 inch wide and equal to the length of the deck.

LIST BASES

Refer to the details on page 16. Lay out the base on the underside of the deck, if necessary. List all the base parts.

Face frames

4 x 97
1 1/4 x 32
1 1/4 x 36
1 1/4 x 25
2 x 42
3 x 42
2 x 38 - 2

4 x 25
1 1/4 x 25
3 3/4 x 42
2 x 42

4 x 56
1 1/4 x 34
1 1/4 x 20
2 x 42
2 x 38
2 x 24

3 x 32
1 1/2 x 32
1 1/4 x 32
2 x 31 1/4 - 2

3 x 13
1 1/2 x 13
1 1/4 x 13
3 3/4 x 31 1/4
2 x 31 1/4

3 x 73
1 1/2 x 73
1 1/4 x 73
3 x 31 1/4
2 x 31 1/4
2 x 4 - 2
2 x 21 1/2 - 2
1 1/2 x 20 - 2

Doors

25 1/2 x 37 1/4 - pr - 2
20 1/2 x 37 1/4
34 1/2 x 19 1/4 - pr.
32 1/2 x 37 1/4 - pr.
36 1/2 x 23 1/4 - pr.
13 1/2 x 22 - 2
36 1/2 x 22 - pr.
32 1/2 x 22 - pr.

Drw Fronts

13 1/2 x 4 1/2 - 2
36 1/2 x 4 1/2 (false)
20 1/2 x 4 1/2
20 1/2 x 5 1/2
20 1/2 x 6 3/4
20 1/2 x 7 3/4
32 1/2 x 4 1/2

Drw Boxes

3 5/8 x 12 3/4 x 22 - 2
3 5/8 x 19 3/4 x "
4 5/8 x 19 3/4 x "
5 7/8 x 19 3/4 x "
6 1/2 x 19 3/4 x "
3 5/8 x 31 3/4 x "

Backs

41 1/8 x 40 1/2
23 1/16 x 40 1/2
36 1/16 x 22 1/2
35 1/16 x 40 1/2
36 5/8 x 26 1/2
28 15/16 x 40 1/2
77 1/8 x 30 5/8
35 1/8 x 30 5/8
41 x 30 5/8

Shelves (pine)

10 5/8 x 39 7/8 - 3
10 5/8 x 22 1/8 - 3
10 5/8 x 34 7/8
10 5/8 x 34 1/8 - 3
10 5/8 x 36 1/4
10 5/8 x 27 3/4

LIST DOORS AND DRAWER FRONTS

Take a look at the various door and drawer-front applications. No doubt you will have chosen one of these applications before this point, but if you haven't, now is the time. The amount of overlay (if any) depends on which option you choose. It also depends on which hinge you are using. Some require various degrees of overlap, so it would be wise to have this information at hand as well. Generally, for an overlay situation, 1/4 inch is commonly used. If your customer prefers to forego the use of pulls and use a built-in bevel on the edges of the fronts instead as finger pulls, you will need a larger overlay because of the bevel. In this case, 1/2 inch all around is necessary. Another very common application is the 3/8-inch lip. Here you rabbet the back edges of the door 3/8 inch by 3/8 inch. Many types of hinges are available for this style and if you start looking closely at your friends' cabinets, you'll notice this application everywhere. Finally, there's the flush inset. This style can have a striking effect but requires a far higher level of skill than the other applications, since flush doors and drawer fronts require a small, consistent gap all around the front. If your face frames or your doors and drawer fronts, for that matter, are even slightly out of square, they become very difficult to fit accurately. If you're not confident in your ability to produce perfectly square face frames and fronts, we recommend that you start out with close to full-size fronts; that is, list them just under the size of the openings and then custom-fit them later. Be prepared to charge a much higher price for this look because of its labor-intensive nature. You can see that the first three styles are far more forgiving and lend themselves more readily to a fast-track production situation.

Once again, just list the overall sizes for now. Later we'll discuss various types of doors, their components, and the construction methods required for each.

TYPES OF DOOR AND DRAWER FRONTS

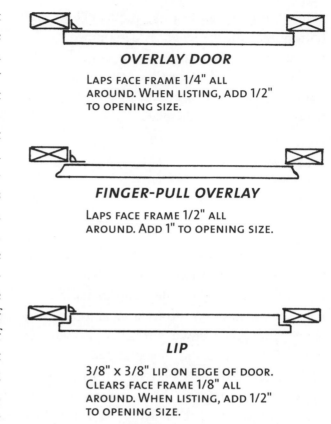

OVERLAY DOOR

LAPS FACE FRAME 1/4" ALL AROUND. WHEN LISTING, ADD 1/2" TO OPENING SIZE.

FINGER-PULL OVERLAY

LAPS FACE FRAME 1/2" ALL AROUND. ADD 1" TO OPENING SIZE.

LIP

3/8" x 3/8" LIP ON EDGE OF DOOR. CLEARS FACE FRAME 1/8" ALL AROUND. WHEN LISTING, ADD 1/2" TO OPENING SIZE.

FLUSH INSET

DOOR SITS IN FACE FRAME OPENING WITH MINIMUM CLEARANCE. WHEN LISTING, SUBTACT 1/16" FROM OPENING SIZE. DOOR IS SANDED TO FIT WHEN HUNG.

LIST DRAWER BOXES

A drawer is a simple box with an attached front. List the number of drawer boxes required for each size. List the width by measuring between the tick-marks indicating the face frame on the deck. Deduct 1 inch from the opening and this will be the width of your box. Most side-mounted drawer slides require 1/2 inch clearance on each side. List the height of the drawer box again by measuring between the tick-marks on your vertical partition. Deduct 1/2 inch from the height of the opening to get the height of the drawer box. Finally, determine the depth of the drawer boxes. For kitchen lower cabinets, a 22-inch drawer is about the deepest that will fit. Drawer slides come in 2-inch increments, so if you decide to put in shorter drawers, be sure to reduce them incrementally as well. For complete details on drawer construction, see Chapter 5.

LIST ROLL-OUTS

Roll-out shelves, as their name implies, are a combination drawer and shelf. They are located behind doors, primarily in lower cabinets. They typically carry heavy items like pots and pans, and should therefore be made from heavier materials than drawers, as discussed later. The width is determined by taking the face-frame opening and subtracting at least 2 inches. The roll-outs are carried on slides that will be blocked out, allowing for door clearance on either side where hinges occur. When the door is open, it still obstructs the opening somewhat and blocks the roll-out from coming out unless this preventative step is taken. Forgetting this detail and over-sizing roll-out shelves is a common error in cabinetmaking. The depth of roll-outs is usually the same as for the drawers. The heights are standard and there's no need to note them at this point. We will also be covering roll-outs in Chapter 5 along with the discussion on doors and drawers.

CASE CUTTING (PART 2) AND BORING

The second phase of cutting involves those parts that you've listed from your decks and partitions. These include the top braces, bases (or toe kicks), backs, and adjustable shelves and bands. Trim the fixed shelves down at this point to make way for the application of your shelf bands. (These bands can be glued and tacked to the shelf edges at any convenient time, but should be done before the parts are stacked so they can be included.) Once the pieces in this second phase have been cut, put them in a convenient location for later stacking and organization.

Drill cabinet ends and partitions for adjustable shelf clips.

JIG FOR DRILLING SHELF HOLES

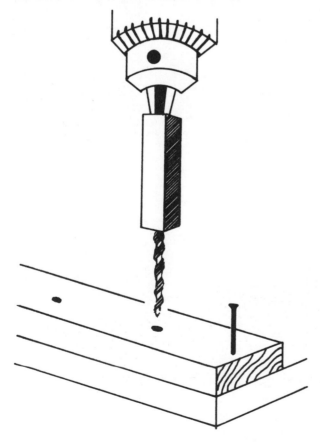

ADJUSTABLE SHELF-HOLE DRILLING JIG

Using a 2-1/4-inch wide piece of hardwood, space 1/4-inch holes every 2 inches, beginning 6 inches from the bottom end. A finish nail pounded into the panel positions the jig and marks the panel bottom for assembly. Hold the other end of the stick with your free hand. The holes in the jig are drilled off-center so that shelf clips on opposite sides of a panel will not obstruct each other and also so that holes will not show right through. Position the jig flush with the panel edge on either side to ensure this. The depth-setting stop is drilled undersized and forced over a 1/4-inch bit. Then it is adjusted to a hole depth of 1/2 inch. A brad-pointed spur bit is recommended for fine work. If you build a lot of cabinets, it is helpful to keep an extra drill set up in this manner.

The use of a line-boring machine will be discussed later in this book, when the subject turns to frameless cabinetry. This machine can also be used here, but for now, the jig offers a perfectly acceptable and economical approach.

ORGANIZING AND STACKING

The way you organize the hundreds of cabinet parts and subassemblies is a critical aspect of shop procedure. Good organization prevents chaos and sets the stage for accurate fabrication.

Parts can be stacked up to 40 or 50 inches high on a dolly (shown below) near the assembly area. Start the stack with a deck, then follow with shelves and their bands in the proper locations. Stack the cabinet partitions and ends next, then add the top braces and base parts. Repeat the arrangement for the next cabinet. The stability of the pile (it can get tall) is improved by stacking the longer cabinets first and by adding spacer blocks (labeled as such to avoid confusion during assembly) wherever necessary.

Stack other subassemblies, backs, doors, drawers, and face frames in distinct bundles in other parts of the shop wherever there is room, but preferably near the assembly area.

A rolling rack (shown at right, discussed on page 70), is particularly useful in organizing frameless cabinetry parts, since they are handled again before assembly and accessability is essential.

LOADED ROLLING RACK

A LIKELY STACK FOR SAMPLE KITCHEN PAGE 29

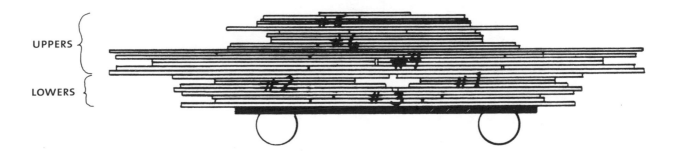

UPPERS

LOWERS

CUTTING AND BORING THE FACE FRAMES

When you use the list of face-frame parts, cutting becomes fairly straightforward. To save time, estimate and rip from 3/4-inch solid wood the approximate lineal footage of each width of stock needed for the entire set.

Cut to length as follows: First, cut the long rails for all the cabinets to minimize waste, then cut the remaining shorter members for each face frame, one frame at a time, stacking the parts for each face frame together on a dolly or table. Face-frame members will eventually be doweled and glued together. In cross-cutting, the saw will leave small tears on one side. It is important to consider this and to keep the chipped cuts to the back of the face frames. This saves sanding and alignment problems later. Also keep an eye out for warped and bowed stock, which should be culled. Watch for flaws, too. The large flaws should be cut away and the small ones kept to the back of the face frame.

The butt joints in face frames are secured with glue and dowels. Two dowels should be used on any joint over 2 inches wide. Joints measuring over 4 inches wide are not recommended where the local climate is subject to radical changes in temperature and humidity.

How you mark the face frames depends on how you will drill them for the dowels. There are two main methods of drilling: the manual doweling jig, detailed here, and the horizontal boring machine, or pocket machine, for which the manufacturer will provide directions.

Whichever method you use, the principal thing to remember is that all the holes must be drilled the same distance from the front surface of the face-frame members. It is economical to mark and bore the entire set of cabinets at one time.

To use the manual doweling jig, arrange the face-frame parts on a flat surface, in the relationship they will have on the cabinet. Referring to opening sizes, written on the plan, mark the locations of adjoining members in their correct positions on the front of the face frame, as shown in the drawing. Then strike a line straight across each joint to indicate the location of the dowel for the jig. Now double-check the opening sizes with those listed on the plan.

TYPICAL FAME-FRAME JOINTS MARKED FOR BORING AND ASSEMBLY

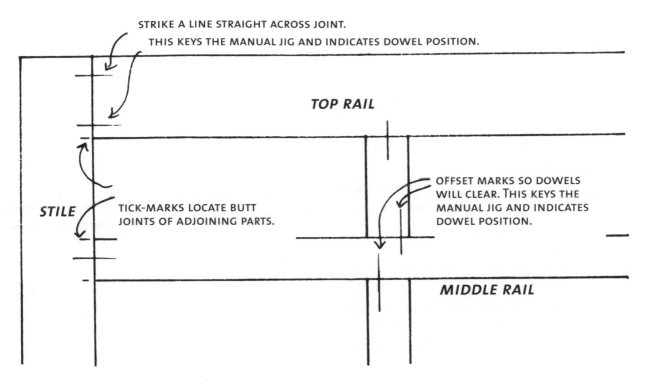

STRIKE A LINE STRAIGHT ACROSS JOINT.
THIS KEYS THE MANUAL JIG AND INDICATES DOWEL POSITION.

TOP RAIL

OFFSET MARKS SO DOWELS
WILL CLEAR. THIS KEYS THE
MANUAL JIG AND INDICATES
DOWEL POSITION.

STILE   TICK-MARKS LOCATE BUTT
JOINTS OF ADJOINING PARTS.

MIDDLE RAIL

CHAPTER 4:

ASSEMBLY

Now that the majority of your cutting has been completed, you're ready to move to what some would consider the fun part. All your careful attention to accuracy and organization will pay off when things come together smoothly. Also, now that the saw is off, you'll be able to hear the radio, which should add even more pleasure to this activity.

Be sure that you have a sturdy workbench on which to assemble your cases. Two or three pieces of particleboard stacked on top of a solid frame are ideal. Be absolutely sure that your bench is level and true. If doors and drawer fronts are installed on a level cabinet to begin with, you'll save a lot of time later in the field by not having to adjust. Your bench should be at a good working height. You might try working at several different heights by adjusting your bench in increments before settling on something permanent. You'll be spending a lot of time at this bench, so it may as well be comfortable.

ASSEMBLING THE FACE FRAME

Gluing together the face frame can be tricky. It must be done quickly, especially in warm weather, since wood glue sets up fast. However, if you cut and bored the frame members accurately, there's no reason why you shouldn't be able to stay well ahead of the game.

Have all the following ready: a large flat surface (the floor will do if no table is available), dowels, glue, a hammer, hardwood pounding blocks and props, pipe clamps, tape measure and carpenter's square, and, of course, all the face-frame parts.

Lay out all the members in place to double-check configuration.

Put glue in all side-grain bored holes. You will learn to gauge the amount that produces just a small amount of squeeze-out around the joint. But remember, better too much glue than not enough. Moving quickly, insert the dowels and tap them in gently. Begin to assemble the face frame, putting glue in the remaining end-grain holes as you go. Note that you should begin assembly from the "inside" of the face-frame configuration, working toward the "outside," as shown in the drawing. The joints are numbered in order of assembly.

FACE-FRAME ASSEMBLY

GLUING SEQUENCE NUMBERED BY JOINT

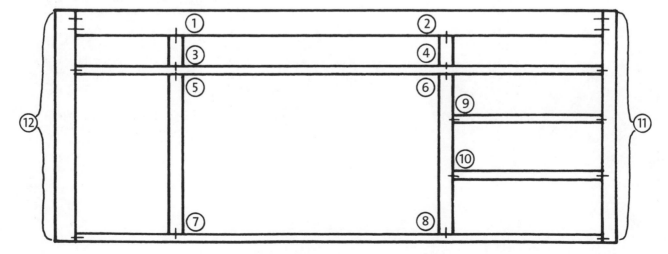

Lay the frame face up on three long pipe clamps (A, B, and C). Tighten up the joints and make sure that the wood is touching the pipes over the entire length. This helps to flatten the face frame, assuming your clamps are straight and not bent. The clamps (D and E) above the face frame should not touch the surface of the wood because the glue in combination with the metal makes an indelible stain that's very difficult to sand off. Use more clamps if the situation calls for them. If the face frame bows up off the pipe clamps, squeeze it back down with c-clamps.

In general, pipe clamps along the length of the face frame are placed below, and clamps across the height are placed on top of the frame.

CLAMPING THE FACE FRAME

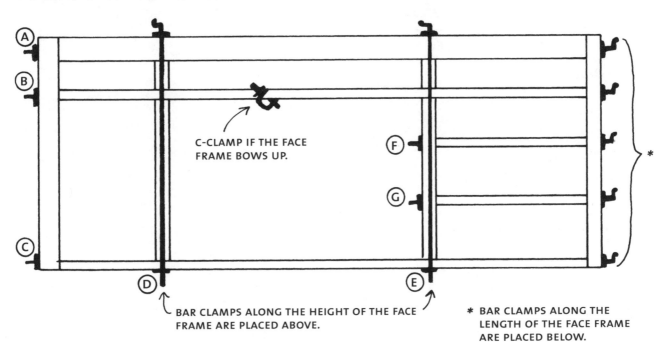

C-CLAMP IF THE FACE FRAME BOWS UP.

BAR CLAMPS ALONG THE HEIGHT OF THE FACE FRAME ARE PLACED ABOVE.

* BAR CLAMPS ALONG THE LENGTH OF THE FACE FRAME ARE PLACED BELOW.

SQUARING A RACKED FRAME

Measure from corner to corner. If the face frame is square, AA will equal BB. The drawing shows a racked frame (exaggerated) where AA is greater than BB. Move the clamps as shown by the arrows and tighten them enough to equalize the measurements. A discrepancy of more than 1/16 inch is not acceptable. This principle can be generalized to correct any racked frame or box.

In theory, careful drilling will produce perfect alignment of the assembled face-frame members, but in fact the face-frame members often ride up or drift a bit from side to side and must be adjusted during clamping, before the glue sets. The dowels will allow about 1/32 inch of play. To make an adjustment, pound on the face frame with a hammer and pounding block and prop, as shown. Be careful—you want to crush the dowel a bit, but if you use too much force you can wind up cracking the dowel or the surrounding wood.

Always place the prop block under the lower member. The block must be long enough to elevate the clamped frame a bit. (Have these blocks cut to size and ready to go before you begin to glue the face frame together). The members can also be adjusted slightly from side to side by pounding with a block. This is especially important around drawer openings and in cabinets where doors and drawers are flush with the face frame. The wood splits easily here so be careful. Measure from opposite corners and square the face frame, if necessary.

DETERMINING SQUARE

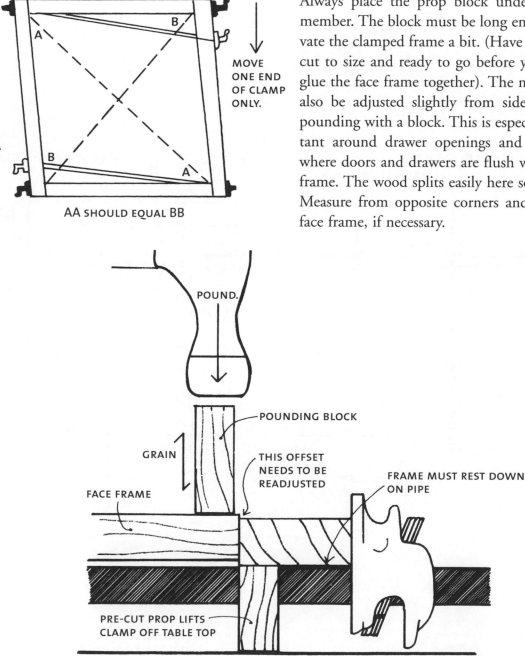

AA SHOULD EQUAL BB

MOVE ONE END OF CLAMP ONLY.

POUND.

POUNDING BLOCK

GRAIN

THIS OFFSET NEEDS TO BE READJUSTED

FRAME MUST REST DOWN ON PIPE

FACE FRAME

PRE-CUT PROP LIFTS CLAMP OFF TABLE TOP

CASE ASSEMBLY

Cabinets, once assembled, are mostly air. During case assembly, the neatly stacked materials really begin to take up space in the shop. From now on you must plan the use of your workspace even more carefully.

It isn't necessary to glue the deck, vertical members, and top braces together. The face frame and back provide sufficient rigidity for cabinetry, which is never moved after being installed.

It is possible to hand-nail during assembly, but the juggling act of trying to hold two plywood panels while pounding and the need to pre-drill all hardwood parts is frustrating and time-consuming. At this point, an air-powered nail gun is one of the most valuable tools a commercial shop can own. While positioning parts with one hand, nails are shot with the other. There is no shock of pounding on the case and the nail is automatically set, even through hardwood face-frame members. The process is many times faster than nailing by hand.

If nailing must be done by hand, pre-position and start as many nails as possible before assembly. Or use Phillips-head sheetrock "grabber" screws, which can also be pre-positioned, driving them with a magnetic tip on a variable speed drill. After building a number of cabinets, both of these methods will soon persuade you to buy a compressor and an air-powered nail gun.

PROCEDURE

The base may be assembled first and set aside, or assembled later when you're ready to attach it to the case.

Working on an assembly table, stand the deck on its back edge. Take a partition that belongs in the middle of the cabinet and stand it on its back edge, at right angles to the deck, and between the appropriate lines on the deck. Making sure the partition and the deck are flat on the assembly table, nail or screw up from the bottom side of the deck in several places.

STEP 1 OF CASE ASSEMBLY

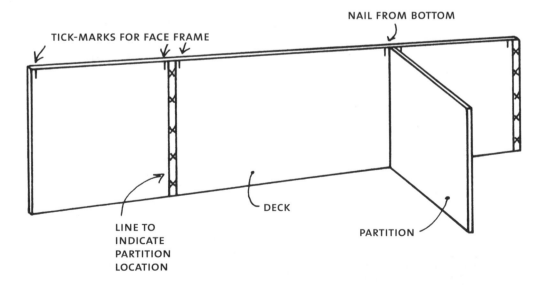

TICK-MARKS FOR FACE FRAME

NAIL FROM BOTTOM

LINE TO INDICATE PARTITION LOCATION

DECK

PARTITION

Repeat this operation for all partitions and wall ends. Finished ends can be fastened to the decks with nails (which are then set, puttied, and sanded), or with screws. When using screws, you must drill 3/8-inch holes (use a brad pointed spur bit) 1/4 inch into the panel. When the screw has been tightened in place, insert a plug of matching wood into the hole and sand flush.

Be careful to keep front edges of the case flush, to provide a uniform plane onto which to glue the face frame.

Stand the assembly upright on the deck. Place the top brace in front of the deck and scribe directly from the partitions, in their exact position, onto the edge of the top brace. Raise it to the top of the partitions without turning it end for end. Place the partitions directly under the tick-marks and fasten with nails down through the top brace. Do the same for the other top brace. This method of locating the top braces ensures that the space between the partitions at the deck is exactly the same as it is at the top braces.

At this time the case may be set aside while building the others, or the face frame may be attached. Either way, the case is weak at this stage and must be flexed as little as possible.

STEP 2 OF CASE ASSEMBLY

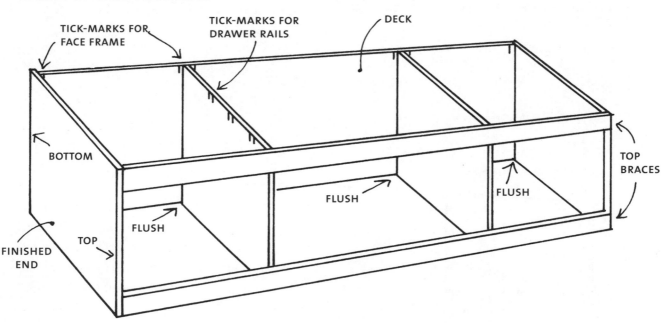

ATTACHING THE FACE FRAME

There are two methods you may use to attach the face frame. Method #1 uses glue only; method #2 uses nails and glue. Each method requires a different assembly sequence, outlined here. Method #1 takes longer because the sequence is more complicated. Additionally, there are no nails through the face frame, which results in a finer appearance. Whenever possible, attach the face frame with glue only. It takes a bit more care and time, but the end product looks better. Method #2 saves time. However, the nail holes must be puttied, and they will show darker when finished. In a cabinet that will be painted, this doesn't matter.

METHOD #1

1. Attach the face frame with glue.
2. Clamp and check the box for squareness.
3. Allow the glue to dry.
4. Remove the clamps.
5. Attach the base.
6. Attach the back.

METHOD #2

1. Attach the base.
2. Attach the back, thereby squaring the box.
3. Attach the face frame with glue and nails. If hand-nailing, you will have to pre-drill hardwood face frames.
4. Fill the nail holes. (There are several types of wood putty available that match various types of wood. Experiment to find one that suits you the best. Some people prefer to fill nail holes after finish has been applied. If you're not doing the finishing, however, the cabinets look better going out to the job if the holes are filled.)

METHOD #1 FACE-FRAME ATTACHMENT

In this process, clamps must reach through the cabinet to hold the face frame securely for several hours. Lay the case on its back on two sawhorses. Place the face frame on the case, checking for correct alignment with tick-marks on the deck. If everything lines up, remove the face frame and have ready an adequate number of clamps. Apply a generous bead of glue along the front edges of the case and spread it with your finger. On a finished end, spread the glue evenly, making sure it reaches the outside edge. Thorough adhesion here is important. Don't worry about drips, because they can be cleaned off after the glue has partially set. Try to avoid using a wet rag on bare wood to wipe up excessive glue. This action will leave a slight residue, which can affect the finish later on. It probably won't be noticeable on cabinet interiors, but it may become apparent on exposed surfaces once a finish is applied.

Now position the face frame over the case as before. (It's good to have help at this point, especially on large cabinets.) Clamping should begin at a lower corner of a finished end (if there is a finished end) or a wall end, and proceed along the entire edge. Clamp wherever needed to make full contact along all the edges, especially along the deck and finished end. Spare no clamps on the latter. Use as many as necessary to get a continuous invisible seam. Never position a face frame below the first veneer of plywood. Later you will be sanding these surfaces flush and if the solid wood is below the veneer, this becomes impossible without sanding through the veneer. Once this happens, you'll know it. It can ruin a perfectly good day.

FACE-FRAME ATTACHMENT METHOD #1

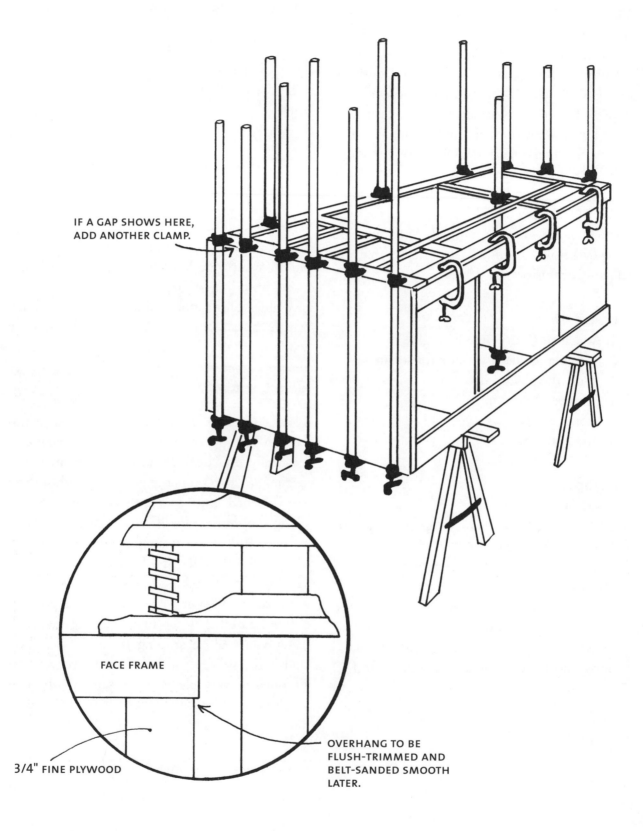

IF A GAP SHOWS HERE,
ADD ANOTHER CLAMP.

FACE FRAME

3/4" FINE PLYWOOD

OVERHANG TO BE
FLUSH-TRIMMED AND
BELT-SANDED SMOOTH
LATER.

METHOD #2 *FACE-FRAME ATTACHMENT*

Method #2 takes advantage of the squaring action of the cabinet back. Attach it first, then apply glue and position the face frame as shown. Nail a finished end first, then nail along the deck (proceeding as numbered on the drawing), making it flush with the face frame. Then nail the rest of the pattern—the order is no longer important. Use as few nails as possible and fill all holes. Clamp any areas that will not lie flat.

ATTACHING THE BACK

Remove all debris from the assembly area that could mar the face frame. Place the cabinet face down and lay the back on it to check for exact fit. Mark the locations of the partitions on the back so that they can be nailed later (with air tools, use staples). Remove the back and spread a small bead of glue on each of the back edges of the cabinet.

Avoid squeeze-outs here, because they are difficult to reach and clean off later. Replace the back on the cabinet. You may need help here also. Begin nailing along an end. Make use of the squareness of the back panel in relationship to the case edges to help true the cabinet. Continue nailing along the deck, shifting the deck and back so that they line up exactly. Then nail along the top brace, all partitions, and ends. Be precise. Every discrepancy now will make hanging doors and drawers more difficult later.

FACE-FRAME ATTACHMENT METHOD #2

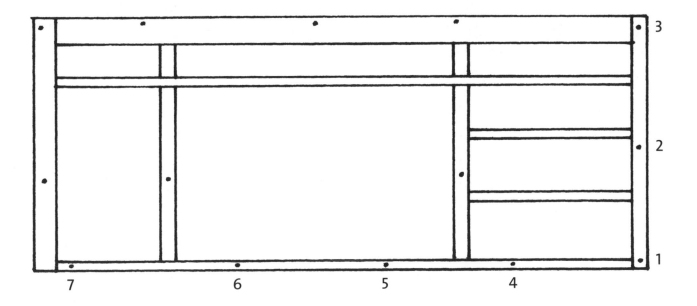

SANDING THE FACE AND FINISHED ENDS

Sanding is one of the most important tasks in the process of cabinetmaking. A poor sanding job can ruin the look of a set no matter how carefully it was constructed.

A good sanding job requires good lighting, because you'll need to check your work from several angles. Minute scratches are elusive, but when stained and finished, they become pronounced. Protect the cabinets with padding when laying them down. Most of all, work with an attitude of poised control. This skill comes with experience and is mostly a matter of touch.

Begin by laying the cabinet on its back or elevate it on saw horses. Bend over the cabinet. Be steady and careful, relax, and let the sander do the work. Use a belt sander with a 120-grit belt.

Move the belt sander back and forth lightly. Take off only enough wood to produce a smooth surface over the joints. Feather out the sanding strokes over a fairly large area, to even out inconsistencies. The idea here is to produce a flat plane so the doors and drawers will fit tightly over the opening on all sides. Remember that total attention while sanding is important. Gouges will result from tilting the sander even slightly. Check for flatness with a straightedge as work progresses.

THE BASICS OF FACE-FRAME SANDING

The work just described has left cross-grain scratches on vertical members as shown. Now approach the same joints with the sanding belt moving from C-C, as shown below. Move the sander back and forth in the direction of C-C, coming as close as possible to the butt joint, but not crossing over so as to leave cross-grain scratches on the horizontal side of the joint. Remember, do not sand off any more wood than necessary and remove wood equally from all parts of the face frame. Practice this technique on a sample frame or utility cabinet before making a good cabinet.

SANDING THE FACE FRAME

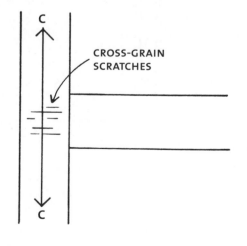

As an example, the face frame for cabinet #3 would be sanded from the inside to the outside of its configuration. Sand all the joints in the order shown in the drawing, ending with the two outside stiles. Make a final check for flatness with a carpenter's square.

Now, using a belt sander, sand the face-frame overhang on the finished ends. Be careful, since the veneer here is very thin (often less than 1/32 inch), and it's easy to sand through the upper layer. If there is much more than a 1/16-inch overhang, remove the excess with a router and trimmer bit—it's more efficient. It helps to draw light pencil lines across the joint about to be sanded. As the marks begin to disappear from the veneer, watch out!

Sand the top front edge of the face frame flush with the top rail. This is not absolutely necessary, but such attention to detail is noticed when the cabinet is delivered, and it enhances your reputation as a careful woodworker. Using a cab-inet scraper, remove the saw marks from the inside edges of the face-frame members. On economy cabinets, both the above procedures can be eliminated; scraping is not necessary on edges that will not show, such as drawer openings and under the middle rail. Always sand and scrape the bottom rail flush with the deck.

For finish-sanding, use a vibrating pad sander. Sand the entire face frame and finished end. Use 120- or 150-grit silicon carbide "A" weight paper. Stack four pieces of paper in the sander simultaneously. As one wears out, tear it off to expose a fresh sheet underneath. Ease all sharp edges both inside and out. Be sure that all sanding marks are eliminated. Examine the butt joints on the face frame from several angles to catch cross-grain scratches. When sanding flat finished ends, move your sander smoothly in long strokes, gradually moving from one side to the other. Quick movements across the grain can result in sanding marks that become visible only when the finish is applied.

SANDING ORDER FOR FACE FRAME

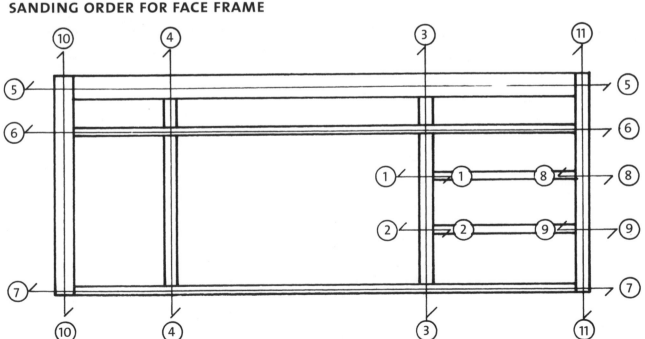

CHAPTER 5:

DOORS, DRAWERS, AND ROLL-OUTS

Doors and drawer fronts provide most of the visual impact of a finished cabinet. Therefore, wood selection becomes extremely important. Grain pattern, color, and the flatness of your material are all things to consider when making this selection. Essentially there are two basic types of fronts—those cut completely from 3/4-inch plywood (flat panel) and those that are made with a frame around a solid lumber or plywood panel (frame and panel).

FLAT-PANEL FRONTS

Doors and drawer fronts cut from 3/4-inch plywood generally offer more of a contemporary look than frame-and-panel cabinets. With flat-panel doors, the grain of the wood becomes the dominant feature and this should be taken into account when cutting. Before cutting, stand your sheets of 4x8 plywood up against the wall and "read the grain." Check for variations, color consistency, and blemishes. You might even take your cut list and roughly lay out your fronts on the plywood with a piece of chalk. It's helpful to refer to your drawings when doing this so you can place certain pieces strategically if you wish.

If you're using a plain sliced panel (this is the result of the log being sliced up into very thin pieces and applied to the plywood substrate in a book-matched fashion), it's nice to balance, or book-match, the grain on a particular door or pair of doors. Grain patterns that seem to peak typically look better when the peaks are turned upward. Book-matching can be a little more expensive, since it generally takes more wood to produce this result. The effect, however, can be striking and will be noticed by most customers.

Flat-panel doors and drawer fronts cut from a continuous sheet of plywood are especially striking in frameless construction where there are no spaces between doors and drawers.

Rotary-cut wood is cut from the log as it spins on a big lathe—the veneer is shaved off in thin layers and applied to the substrate. Regardless of your choice of veneer, it's important to match the grain as best you can, cutting the doors and drawer fronts from a continuous piece as shown in the drawing. Note that you're limited to a width of 48 inches if you want to cut your fronts

FLAT-PANEL FRONT

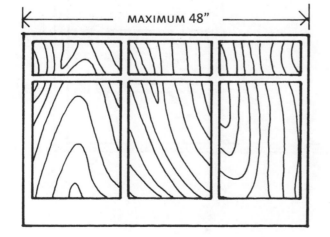

out of a single piece, but often you'll be able to match everything closely if you pay attention. Be sure to label the pieces as they come off the saw, indicating their orientation as well as their ultimate position on the cabinet.

When ordering plywood for the fronts, you might specify matched panels. This means that the wood is cut from the same log in sequence. It usually is no more expensive, since the panels are produced in sequence anyway, and it's simply a matter of picking them carefully.

Note that any edge can be applied to any door regardless of the type. If you use one of the shaped edges as shown here, for more expensive cabinets it would be better to apply a solid wood edge around plywood doors first before routing the detail. Otherwise the core of the panel, which isn't particularly good looking, will become more prominent. Sand the edges with a vibrating sander very carefully to maintain consistency. When sanding the face, use long strokes, moving from top to bottom while gradually moving across the face of the panel.

SHAPED EDGE TREATMENTS

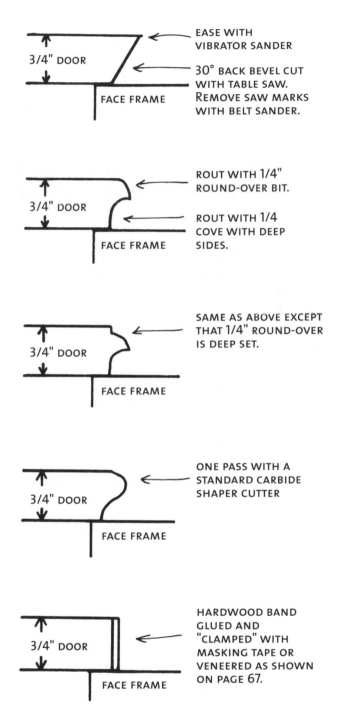

EASE WITH VIBRATOR SANDER

30° BACK BEVEL CUT WITH TABLE SAW. REMOVE SAW MARKS WITH BELT SANDER.

ROUT WITH 1/4" ROUND-OVER BIT.

ROUT WITH 1/4 COVE WITH DEEP SIDES.

SAME AS ABOVE EXCEPT THAT 1/4" ROUND-OVER IS DEEP SET.

ONE PASS WITH A STANDARD CARBIDE SHAPER CUTTER

HARDWOOD BAND GLUED AND "CLAMPED" WITH MASKING TAPE OR VENEERED AS SHOWN ON PAGE 67.

FRAME-AND-PANEL FRONTS

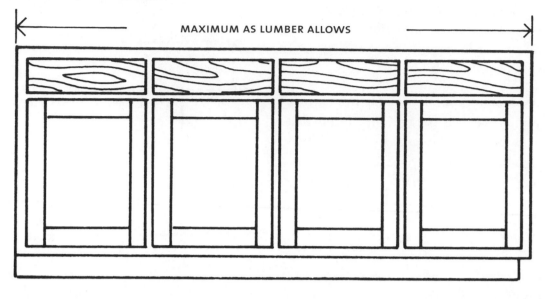

MAXIMUM AS LUMBER ALLOWS

FRAME-AND-PANEL FRONTS

With frame-and-panel construction, the drawer fronts (especially the top drawers) are generally too small to accommodate frames and panels. In this case, a solid piece of lumber is used for the drawer fronts. It's nice to cut these fronts from a single board, while matching the grain from left to right. The series is limited to the length of

A FRAME-AND-PANEL FRONT

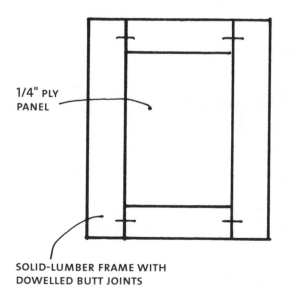

1/4" PLY PANEL

SOLID-LUMBER FRAME WITH DOWELLED BUTT JOINTS

your available wood, but most runs are not that long. As with veneer selection, try to choose your wood carefully, for this is where the ultimate look will be achieved.

Frame-and-panel door construction generally lends itself to a more traditional feel. The variations are endless and a little creativity will go a long way to set your cabinets apart from the norm. Frame-and-flat-panel doors are those where a 1/4-inch plywood panel is set into a solid-wood frame, whereas frame-and-raised panel doors include a solid-wood panel shaped to fit within the frame. Various widths of stiles and rails, and the use of arches, contrasting woods, and edge details, are all elements that can be used to produce distinctive looking cabinets.

It's particularly important to be diligent about maintaining flatness during door construction. Choose wood for your frames that is straight and true. Sight each piece and if you detect a slight bow here and there, place the crown outward.

A simple, economical 3/8-inch lip frame-and-panel door can be made as follows. First make up the frames, joining the stiles and rails together with dowels or mortise-and-tenon joints. Then attach a 1/4-inch piece of plywood to the back with glue and brads. With a shaper, router, or table saw, cut a 3/8-inch by 3/8-inch rabbet around the perimeter. Sand the face and ease all sharp edges. Another variation of this same idea is to cut a 1/4-inch rabbet with a router into the back inside edge of the frame. Carefully fit a 1/4-inch piece of plywood into the rabbet. You will either need to chisel each corner of the rabbet to make it square or round off the corners of your plywood to fit, since the router will leave rounded corners.

Most of the time, grooves are cut along the inside of the door frame to accommodate the panel. If you're doweling your frame together, you'll need to stop the grooves short of the end of the stiles or vertical members of the door. A version of a mortise-and-tenon joint is fairly easy to make on the table saw. Cut your horizontal members 3/4 inch longer than the inside edge of your frame. Then run 1/4-inch grooves on the inside edges of all four pieces of your door frame, 3/8 inch deep. Finally cut 3/8-inch long tenons on each end of the rails or horizontal pieces with the table saw exactly in line with the grooves. This takes some practice, but once you get the hang of it, you'll find that this is a very easy and practical way to make door frames.

FRAME-AND-PANEL CONSTRUCTION

SIDE VIEW

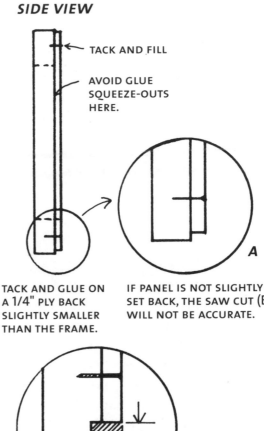

TACK AND FILL

AVOID GLUE SQUEEZE-OUTS HERE.

A

TACK AND GLUE ON A 1/4" PLY BACK SLIGHTLY SMALLER THAN THE FRAME.

IF PANEL IS NOT SLIGHTLY SET BACK, THE SAW CUT (B) WILL NOT BE ACCURATE.

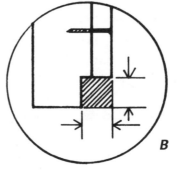

B

ONE SAW SETTING AND 8 PASSES THROUGH THE SAW REMOVE A 3/8"x3/8" RABBET ALL AROUND THE DOOR (OR USE A 3/8" SHAPER CUTTER).

A FRAME WITH A GROOVE RECEIVES A 1/4" PLYWOOD OR SOLID PANEL.

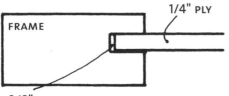

FRAME

1/4" PLY

3/8" GROOVE

ROUTED RABBET

THE RABBET IS ROUTED ON THE BACK SIDE OF THE FRAME AFTER IT IS ASSEMBLED. THE 1/4" PANEL MUST FIT PERFECTLY.

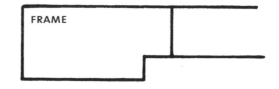

FRAME

RAISED-PANEL CONSTRUCTION

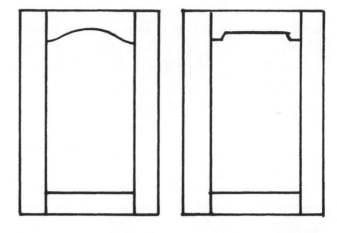

Frame-and-raised-panel doors are made essentially the same way, except that the panel is machined from solid lumber. You can make a simple raised panel using the table saw, or if your budget allows, use a shaper with raised panel cutters. Be sure to allow some room for wood movement within the frame, as solid wood will expand and contract with variations in temperature and humidity.

Arches at the tops of the doors can add a classical appearance to cabinets. Lay out your curves very carefully—even subtle variations can completely change the look of a door. Pay particular attention to overall proportion and literal symmetry. You can use a flexible ruler or other springy material and three hands to draw simple curves. Trace your final pattern on one side of the centerline and transfer it to the other so that both sides match exactly. Make templates for commonly used details and save them for future reference. A circle template or simply the bottoms of putty or paint containers work well for striking various radii.

VARIATIONS IN TOP AND BOTTOM RAILS

BELOW ARE A FEW VISUAL SUGGESTIONS THAT ALLOW STYLING VARIATIONS.

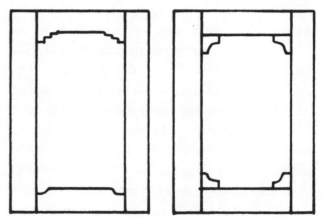

CUTTING AN ARCH

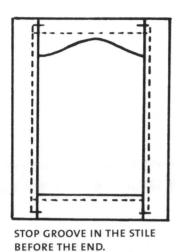

STOP GROOVE IN THE STILE
BEFORE THE END.

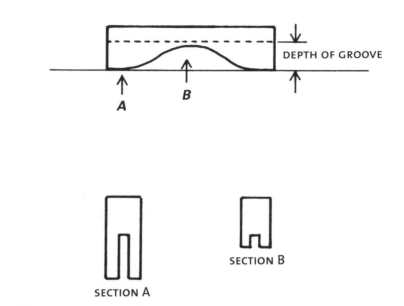

DEPTH OF GROOVE

SECTION A

SECTION B

Cut the arches in the rails with a band saw or a good quality saber saw. Scrape and/or sand the cuts smooth, taking care not to alter the integrity of the curve. The groove in the frame can be cut using a 1/4-inch carbide slotting router bit, which will follow the pattern. The panel size in the curved section must then be estimated by tracing the curve on the panel and adding 5/16 inch or so. The groove can also be cut on the table saw, but you'll have to set the blade about 3/8 inch higher than the highest point of the curve. This allows the use of a square panel without having to fit the panel to the curve. Obviously this method works only with a flat panel.

MANUFACTURED DOORS

Since door making is considered one of the most labor intensive aspects of cabinetmaking, you might consider purchasing your doors from a cabinet door manufacturer. They will make any size door you need (within their guidelines). There will typically be many styles to choose from, and since a company's volume is often very high, prices can be quite competitive. Weigh these prices against your projected time and material costs, and you'll probably be surprised at what you discover.

DRAWERS

The ease with which the drawers operate can make or break a set of cabinets. One of the first things customers do when they see their new cabinets for the first time is to open the drawers and test their motion. It's important that the drawers operate smoothly. It's also critical that they're built well, since they'll get a lot of use during their lifetime.

European slides, as they're called, are recommended for average use. They're reasonably priced, durable, and since most of them are epoxy-coated, they are quiet. A big step up would be to use a full-extension, progressive-action, ball-bearing slide, but they are pricey. For top quality cabinets, however, the price is worth it. There are many, many types of drawer slides to choose from and each has its own characteristics so it's wise to do a fair amount of research in this area before settling on your standard.

The material for drawer boxes is usually 1/2 inch thick, but the type of material itself can vary. Many people like to use 9-ply birch plywood, sometimes referred to as Baltic birch or apple plywood. This is a nice looking material with no voids and can be quite attractive when the edges are sanded with care. Other people prefer solid lumber, which is more expensive but gives a high quality look. If the cabinet interiors are melamine, you may wish to stay with the same material for the drawers. In this case, consider using Confirmat assembly screws for fastening. If these screws are used, choose 3/4-inch thick material for the fronts and backs to avoid splitting the wood. Confirmat fasteners are described later in the section on frameless cabinetry.

The drawer box is simply that—a four-sided box with the drawer front attached. Before you can list your drawer box parts, however, you'll need to decide which type of joinery you intend to use. The most economical is a butt joint—simply butt the fronts and backs to the sides. Other options are to rabbet the fronts and backs into the sides, or dovetail the parts together. In each case, you'll need to determine how much to subtract from the overall width of your drawer boxes to get the length of your fronts and backs. Don't forget to allow for the drawer slides as well. If you're using side-mounted slides, they almost always require 1/2 inch on each side, but sometimes it's wise to deduct another 1/16 inch for good measure. It's better to have the drawer too loose than too tight. The length of the sides, as we mentioned earlier, should be sized in 2-inch increments to fit your slides. The 1/4-inch drawer bottom is grooved into the drawer sides as shown with 1/16-inch of tolerance, which allows for squaring of the drawer box during assembly. As an option, the front and back can be sized the same height as the sides, in which case you would need to groove these pieces, too. The length of the drawer bottom would, of course, have to be adjusted downward as well.

If you are dovetailing your drawers together, all parts will need to be the same height. Many of the European drawer slides wrap around the bottom of the drawer side, in which case the drawer bottom can merely be applied to the bottoms of the sides, fronts, and backs. The drawer bottom is then cut to the overall size of the drawer. Since the drawer slide wraps around the box, the side edges of the drawer bottom are hidden. The front edge of the drawer bottom is, of course, hidden behind the finished drawer front.

DRAWER CONSTRUCTION DETAILS

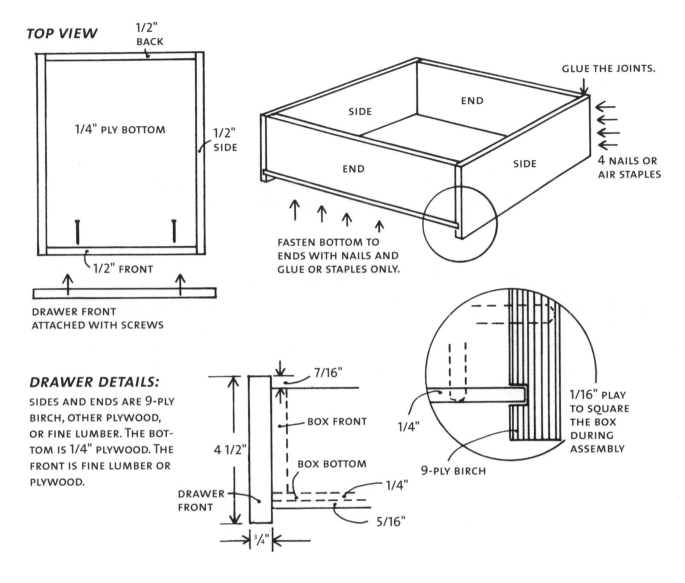

TOP VIEW

1/2" BACK

1/4" PLY BOTTOM

1/2" SIDE

1/2" FRONT

DRAWER FRONT ATTACHED WITH SCREWS

GLUE THE JOINTS.

SIDE

END

END

SIDE

4 NAILS OR AIR STAPLES

FASTEN BOTTOM TO ENDS WITH NAILS AND GLUE OR STAPLES ONLY.

DRAWER DETAILS:

SIDES AND ENDS ARE 9-PLY BIRCH, OTHER PLYWOOD, OR FINE LUMBER. THE BOTTOM IS 1/4" PLYWOOD. THE FRONT IS FINE LUMBER OR PLYWOOD.

7/16"

BOX FRONT

BOX BOTTOM

4 1/2"

DRAWER FRONT

1/4"

5/16"

3/4"

1/4"

9-PLY BIRCH

1/16" PLAY TO SQUARE THE BOX DURING ASSEMBLY

ROLL-OUTS

Roll-out shelves generally carry more weight than drawers, and should be built accordingly: 5/8-inch or 3/4-inch thick bottoms are recommended, especially if you think they will carry pots and pans or mixing bowls. There are a variety of ways to make roll-outs; we've shown a simple pine box with a bottom nailed and glued inside the front, back, and sides. Note how the front extends about 7/16 inch beyond the sides. This is to help obscure the front of the drawer slide. It's not really necessary, but adds a nice touch. Some cabinetmakers use high roll-out backs, short fronts, and sides that are contoured to match. This helps to prevent things from falling off the back when the roll-out is extended. The main point to remember is that roll-outs can be made in several different configurations, and, with a little experimenting, you'll come up with a standard that suits you.

HANGING DRAWERS AND ROLL-OUTS

A drawer that is mounted properly moves easily with no tightness and a minimum of play, does not rock in its tracks, stays closed at all times, and fits squarely up against the cabinet. Before you hang the drawers, set the cabinet up on your bench at a comfortable working height, and level it from front to back and from side to side. The cabinet will be installed plumb and square and consequently the care that you take here will be reflected after installation.

In face-frame cabinets, spacer blocks are required to build out the partition flush with the opening of the face frame. For roll-outs, these spacer blocks will need to be even thicker so that the roll-out clears the door and/or hinges. You

may have to glue together several pieces of wood to achieve the necessary thickness. Sometimes it's easier to mount the drawer slides to the spacer blocks first and then install this assembly in the cabinet all at once. Tack this assembly into place and test-fit the drawer or roll-out. If it's too tight, remove the assembly and sand or plane the back of the spacer accordingly. Conversely, if the drawer is too loose, add cardboard or plastic laminate shims behind the spacer until you have a perfect fit. Here is where all the care taken in cutting and assembly will pay off. If everything is true and square, the drawers will pop painlessly into place.

Once the drawers are installed, attach the finished drawer fronts to the drawer boxes with screws from the inside of the drawer. Be sure that all the fronts are mounted with the same margins around the drawer boxes. This will ensure that everything lines up when viewed from the front.

HANGING THE DOORS

Mount all the hinges on the doors at the same time. Depending on the type of hinges that are used, and the help you have available, the doors can be hung while the cabinet is either upright on the bench or on its back. If the hinges are mounted to the face frame from the front and you're working alone, you might want to lay the cabinet down on its back to make use of gravity. Level the cabinet again before you install the doors. Be sure that the doors are lined up with the drawers above and that you end up with even gaps all around. Another method is to clamp a stick along the bottom edge of the face frame to act as an alignment mechanism and as a support for the doors if you're installing them upright.

Occasionally you may run into a door that has become warped for one reason or another. Try putting a block between the door and the cabinet and clamping the opposite corner to the cabinet. Leave the setup overnight. Sometimes this gentle act of persuasion can produce the desired result of flattening out the door.

If the pulls have been selected before this time, drill holes for the pull screws in both the drawer fronts and the doors before the cabinet is removed from the bench. Again, the use of a simple drilling template will save a lot of time.

ROLL-OUT CONSTRUCTION

TOP VIEW WITH DOORS OPEN

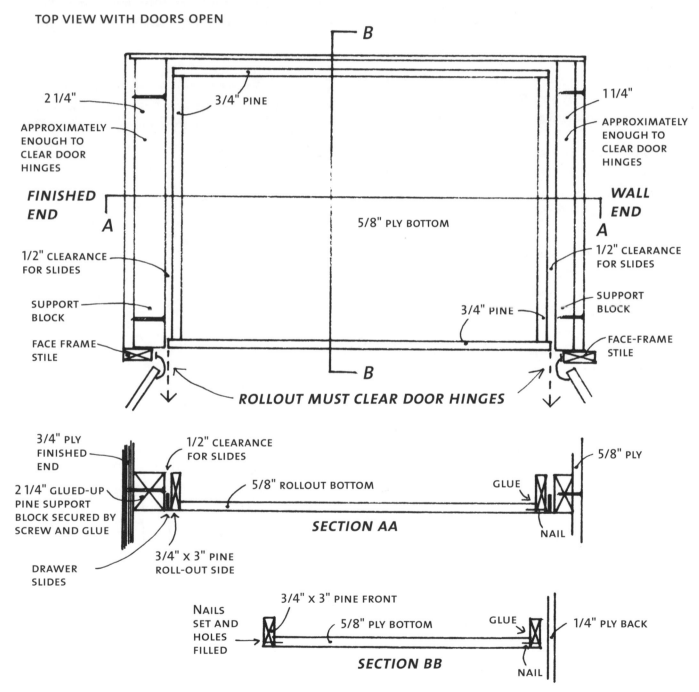

CHAPTER 6:

FRAMELESS CABINETRY

Some of the differences between frameless and face-frame cabinetry were summarized in the introduction to this book. Perhaps the two most noteworthy advantages of the frameless system are the space-saving nature of the design and the savings in time and material over face-frame construction. Space efficiency is realized primarily in drawers and roll-outs. Since there are no face frames taking up room, the drawers and roll-outs are sized larger and are mounted directly on the partitions. It may not seem like much, but the cumulative effect can be significant.

The use of face-frame construction gained popularity in this country many years ago. Early American cabinetmakers used face frames for fashion and style. (Thus the word "stile" came to be used for the vertical members of the face frames.) Wood was plentiful in those days, and, to some degree, still is. In Europe, however, much of the wood was used up by the time World War II was over. In addition, cabinet-makers at the time were faced with the challenge of providing a massive amount of casework for all the structures that needed to be rebuilt after the war. As a result, an ingenious modular system of frameless cabinetmaking was developed. Widely used in Europe, the frameless system is rapidly gaining popularity in this country.

TOOLING CONSIDERATIONS

A good table saw is one of the most useful and versatile tools that exists. I would say that if you are limited in space and a vertical panel saw is not an option, spend some money and get a Delta Unisaw, a Powermatic, or something equivalent with at least a 5-horsepower motor and a good fence. Build a nice sturdy table around the saw and you'll find that this will become your work center. Everything starts around accurate cutting, so don't skimp on this tool.

You'll probably find that most plywood or flat stock is not exactly square when you buy it, so you may want to make a carriage for squaring up your blanks once you've cut them. As long as you've managed to get two edges at 90° to each

TABLE-SAW CARRIAGE

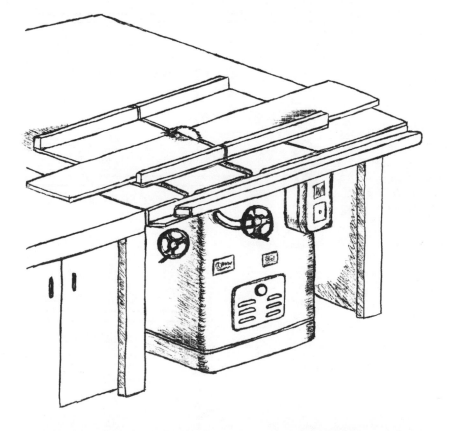

LINE-BORING MACHINE

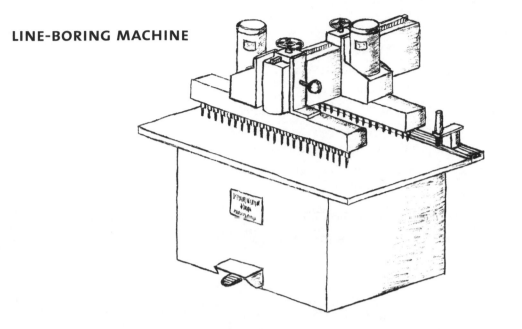

other, the table saw will do the rest. Never use a factory edge for a finished edge, as factory edges usually get a little hammered during the shipping and handling process, and consequently won't take edge-banding very well.

Another essential tool for building frameless cabinets is some type of boring machine. This could be limited to a drill press, which would then be used exclusively for drilling the 35mm holes in the doors for the special European hinges. However, a line-boring machine, sometimes referred to as a multi-spindle boring machine, saves an enormous amount of time by simultaneously drilling two sets of parallel holes down the inside face of the cabinet side or partition.

Line drilling isn't essential for the manufacture of frameless cabinets. All the hardware comes drilled for both the use of system screws and for conventional screws. Holes for adjustable shelves can be drilled using the method shown on page 40 and the hardware placed on the cabinet sides with regular screws. This takes a lot more time because of the lack of registration that line-boring offers, but is certainly a workable alternative.

To call yourself a frameless cabinetmaker, you'll need some type of an edge-bander. Since there are no face frames involved, the raw edges of your

cabinet components need to be covered with something. This is what an edge-bander does.

In its simplest form, your edge-bander could be a $2 iron from your local thrift shop. You can buy pre-glued edge-banding in rolls—it comes in most common wood veneers as well as in a number of vinyl colors to match a variety of laminates. To apply the banding, you merely heat up your iron and press the stuff on. The iron melts the glue and causes it to stick to the edge.

**IRON-ON APPLICATION
OF EDGE-BANDING**

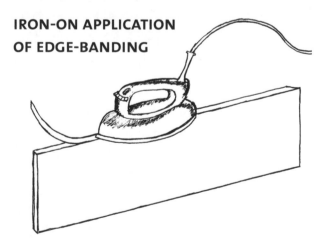

Applying edge-banding can be tricky and takes a little practice to get right. Typical mistakes are using too much heat and scorching the edge-banding, or leaving the iron on too long. The idea is to use just enough heat to melt the glue, then back off and rub across the top of the banding with a hammer head or some other steel object to draw out the heat quickly and set the glue. (You need to apply plenty of pressure while doing this.) There are hand-trimmers available to not only trim the ends of the part that you are edge-banding but also to trim the excess material from along the two edges. Again, these take a little getting used to, but they are quite effective. A regular file is useful to soften the edge. Clean up excess glue with a solvent.

TAPED-ON EDGING

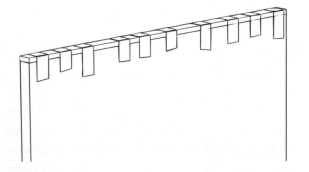

Another edge-banding option is to cut up some thin strips of wood and glue them directly to the edges with yellow glue, using strips of masking tape to hold them until the glue dries. You'll need to go back and belt-sand the saw marks off the faces, and also trim the excess off the edges as well. A razor-sharp chisel laid flat works well for this purpose. Obviously, this option is best for those for whom time is no object.

The next step up from an iron is a bench model edge-bander. These can cost anywhere from one to five thousand dollars. Two types are available. There is a hot-air machine (this type of machine has shown itself to be inferior and troublesome), which uses preglued edge-banding. The other type of edge-bander has a glue pot to which you add special glue pellets. Since the pellets are available in different colors, they can help disguise the fine glue line between your panel and its edge-banding. Some very reliable and afford-

able edge-banders of this nature have recently been developed, and if you plan to do any kind of edge-banding volume, this tool will be well worth your while. As a point of reference, high-volume-production edge-banders can sell for many thousands of dollars, depending on the number of bells and whistles. Some are capable of applying anything from a veneer edge up to a piece of 3/4-inch by 1-1/2-inch hardwood, while trimming both edges and the ends at the same time. Just be aware that these machines can be very sensitive and require a lot of tinkering to keep them running properly.

LAYOUT AND CUT-LISTING

Frameless cabinets are typically divided up into modules. That is, each cabinet bay is a separate component, and once they are connected together they comprise a single run of cabinets. This approach has certain advantages. One is that smaller units are much easier to move and, as a result, one person can often stock an entire job with cabinets (using dollies) and install them with no help. Another advantage is that hinging and door sizing remain consistent throughout the job, which greatly reduces the margin of error. Incidentally, despite the mind-boggling variety of hinges available for frameless cabinets, you only need to stock a couple of types—this reduces inventory and helps you avoid a certain amount of head-scratching. We've chosen to limit our use to two types of full-overlay hinges: a clip-on, self-closing type with a 125° swing (for typical applications), and a zero-protrusion hinge (designed to move completely out of the way at 90° to allow for roll-out drawers to pass the door, thus eliminating the need for any kind of build-out). If European hinge engineering intrigues you, then you'll be guaranteed many hours of entertainment trying to figure out which hinge does what, while in the meantime

A SET OF FRAMELESS CABINETS

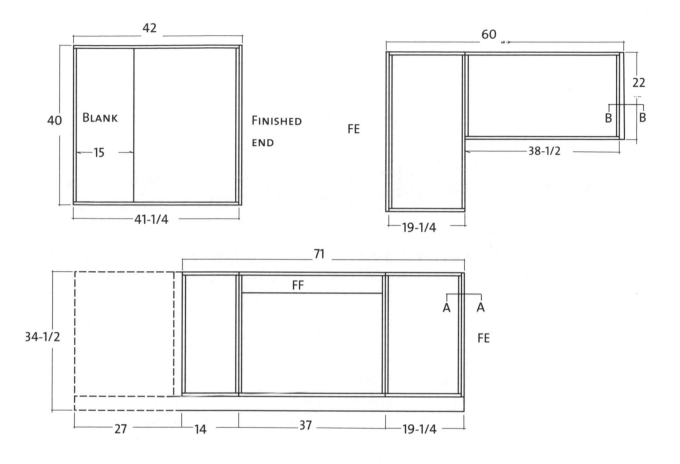

comparing different manufacturers. The layout and cut-listing of a set of frameless cabinets is far easier than for a set of face-frame cabinets, simply because there's no face frame to worry about. Begin by deciding how you want to divide up your modules. For simplicity, we'll use the same layout pictured on page 29. When drawing the sketches, it's best to double up the lines to show the actual components. This way it becomes clear how pieces butt together. It makes the listing of parts far more foolproof.

We should add here that it isn't absolutely essential to break up your cabinets into individual modules. It is possible to have a continuous deck with several partitions mounted to it. However, this approach is more complex for a couple of

reasons. Half-overlay hinges are required where two doors are mounted to the same partition, which increases your inventory of hinges and/or hinge plates. It also complicates the layout process, increasing the likelihood of error when it comes to listing the sizes of your doors and drawer fronts. We've found that the few additional partitions required to build individual modules is a small price to pay for the advantages gained in using a modular approach. Also, as we said, you have the added advantage of smaller units and the efficiency in handling that goes with them. We will assume that for the purposes of this book, we will be using the modular approach.

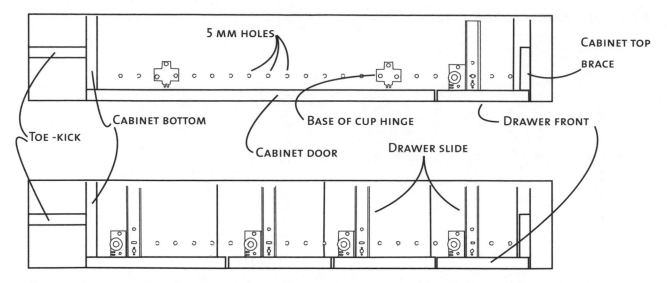

FULL-SIZE TEMPLATES: DRILL A ROW OF 5MM HOLES SPACED 32 MM APART. DRAW THE CABINET LAYOUT FULL-SIZE ON THE TEMPLATE STOCK. TRACE THE HINGES AND DRAWER SLIDES.

FULL-SIZE TEMPLATES

The heights take a bit more figuring, but this can be simplified by using full-size templates showing several door and drawer configurations along with their respective hardware locations. Create a template from a piece of 6-inch wide 1/4-inch plywood; cut it a few inches longer than the cabinet height. Bore a row of 5mm holes exactly 32mm apart center to center (or use a line-boring machine). Draw in the top and bottom of the cabinet partition, centering the series of holes on the partition. When the partitions are cut and bored, they become "balanced panels," since the holes are centered from top to bottom. This makes them reversible, eliminating the risk of installing them upside down.

TOE-KICKS

The toe kick, or base, is often built to accommodate several boxes or a complete run of cabinets. Toe-kicks for frameless cabinets are really no different than those for face-frame cabinets. They're best built of plywood. Over time, excessive water could cause a particleboard base to swell, which would jeopardize the integrity of

the cabinets. Plywood is far more stable, and there is usually plenty of plywood scrap around the shop to recycle into toe-kicks.

Usually the toe-kick is around 3 inches shallower than the cabinet above it, including the applied finished material, although that number isn't set in stone. We usually hold the toe-kick back from the wall a little, which allows more flexibility in final placement. Many times toe-kicks are taken out to the job separately and installed square and level before the cabinets go in. The thinking is that it's easier to level a small object than a large one. Once you have a level platform to work on, installing the cabinets becomes relatively painless. A few nails or screws down through the top of the deck lock everything in place. Once the cabinets are installed, the toe-kick is faced with a finish material (Appendix 4, page 79).

SCRIBES

Wall scribes can be done in one of two ways as shown, depending on the look you're after. These are usually made out of the same materials as your doors. They're typically shipped loose to the job site and applied to the cabinet after installation. It's a good idea to make them about 1/4 inch wider than they calculate out to be, particularly for a wall-to-wall situation. Merely set your cabinet in the center of the opening and then fit your scribes accordingly. If you wish to avoid nails through the face, you can either nail the scribes from inside the cabinet or simply glue them to the stop blocks behind.

APPLIED FINISH ENDS

Exposed ends of cabinets obviously need to be finished. We've found that the easiest way to achieve this is to apply a panel with screws from the inside of the cabinet. Add these panels to your door list and make them at the same time. The finished ends often match the doors themselves and the look can be quite elegant if an outside detail is routed on both as shown.

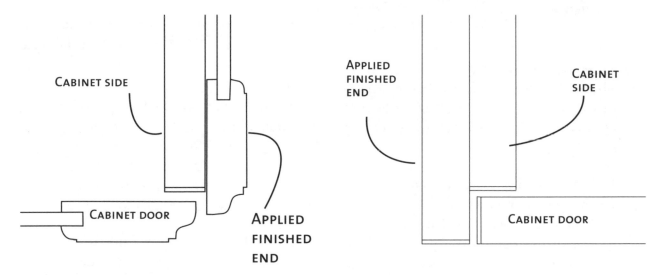

APPLIED FINISHED ENDS: FACE-FRAME CABINET WITH TRADITIONAL DETAILING, LEFT, AND FRAMELESS CABINET, RIGHT.

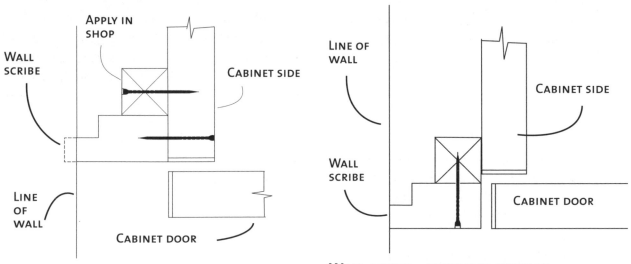

WALL SCRIBE

WALL SCRIBE - OPTIONAL METHOD

ORGANIZING YOUR CUTTING

Before turning on the saw, take time to optimize your cutting. Draw a rectangle on a piece of paper to simulate a 4x8 piece. Block out the parts, showing your cutting plan. Time devoted now to planning can save lots of material later.

Once you begin cutting, label each part or stack of identical parts shortly after it leaves the saw. Otherwise you'll find yourself re-measuring parts to find the one you're looking for. During the planning process, assign each cabinet a number. Then, while you're cutting, write that number on an edge of the part that corresponds to the cabinet. Also add an abbreviation to identify the part. For example, the deck of cabinet #1 would carry the label 1-D; a shelf for cabinet #3 would be labeled 3-S.

Label all the vertical parts on the top front edge and all the horizontal parts on the back, somewhere in the center. Make a quick inspection at this point and choose the best edge for the front. A little chipping on a cabinet back won't matter, but it would on the front. You will automatically know that you need to band the edge adjacent to the label on the vertical parts and the opposite edge on the horizontal parts. In the event that the partitions are not reversible, you'll always be in good shape by keeping the label on top.

Since frameless cabinets are typically built in modules, their parts are usually shorter and so it's easier to stack the parts vertically rather than horizontally. Keep all the labels facing out so the parts can be quickly identified. Since you'll be handling each part at least one more time, it's important that everything is organized and accessible. A rolling rack with several tiers (see page 41) is handy for stocking and transporting parts from one station to the other.

APPLYING EDGE-BANDING

Depending on your equipment, this operation can be quick or laborious. Here's where labeling pays off. At a glance, you'll be able to determine which edge gets banded. Don't take the time to detail the banded edges at this point--just apply the edge-banding and replace the part on the rack. Make sure to keep all like parts together.

BORING THE HOLES

Next, punch the 5mm holes with the line-boring machine. You will have already determined your boring pattern, and it's simply a matter of setting up your stops and going for it. Here, too, if you have a multi-spindle boring machine, this operation will take only a few minutes to perform. If you're drilling each panel by hand, one hole at a time (p 40), it's a different story. You'll probably miss your favorite TV program that night if you're working under a deadline.

Note that the distance of the first row of holes from the edge-banded front of the panel is always 37mm. Make sure the rear set of holes is also located properly, to take advantage of the pre-drilled holes in the drawer slides. Remember that all your slides and hinge plates will be mounted at these holes using system screws, which are just wide-diameter screws that thread directly into the 5mm holes. If you always stay with a consistent depth and use the same length of drawer slide this won't change. But in reality, this is dreaming. There are always custom situations to adapt to, but you'll find that standardization equals profits every step of the way.

BUILDING DOORS AND DRAWERS

At this stage you may want to build your doors and drawers. They can be built at any stage, but one advantage of doing them before assembly is that you can install them right after the cabinet is built. This way you only lift the cabinet off your bench once—complete. There's something satisfying about having everything come together at one time and in one place. Assuming you've done your homework properly, this will happen. Then again, if you didn't, well, we all have a stash of nice cabinet doors up in the loft that we're sure we'll use up someday.

ASSEMBLY

Pull off the cart all the cabinet parts you will need for assembling the first case. Detail all the banded edges, that is, sand or ease the sharp edges that occur during the edging process. If you've applied all the edges by hand, chances are that the parts are ready to go. If you used an automatic edge-bander, this detailing may or may not have happened as part of the process. The point is that it's easier to detail before the cabinet is assembled rather than afterward.

Reference your layout templates and begin installing drawer slides and hinge plates on the partitions. Consider installing all the hardware on all the partitions at this time since you've got the screw gun in your hand. But be sure to detail the banding ahead of time, as it's difficult to do once the hardware is mounted. Stand the outfitted partitions up nearby and grab them when you're ready to integrate them into the cabinets.

Start out by pinning the components together using 1-1/2-inch nails from a pneumatic nail gun. Drop back and pre-drill for the Confirmats, using three or four of them along a typical 24-inch length. Special stepped drill bits are made to be used with these fasteners, but

CONFIRMAT FASTENER

THESE BIG SCREWS HAVE A COARSE THREAD AND ARE MADE FOR USE IN PANEL ASSEMBLY. THEY WORK WELL BOTH IN PLYWOOD AND MDF- OR PARTICLEBOARD-CORE MATERIALS.

they're expensive and break easily since they're pure carbide. We've found that a 15/64-inch bit with a 1/2-inch countersink works just fine at a fraction of the cost. One fastener is sufficient in the center of the top rail of the lowers in conjunction with a nail on either side to keep it from twisting. Hold the fasteners at least 2 inches shy of the edges to avoid splitting. Keep a separate drill chucked up with your pre-drill bit (a pneumatic drill works well). Insert fasteners in all the holes at the same time and then drive them in with a screw gun one after the other. This is a small example of how you can accrue time savings by repeating the same activity as often as possible before moving on to another.

Staple the back on, flip the cabinet up, pop in the drawers (and roll-outs, if any), clip on the doors, and mount the finished end if there is one. (Remember that if you have roll-outs in a cabinet, you should have used zero-protrusion hinges on their corresponding doors.) Take a 1/8-inch thick spacer about 1 inch wide and place this spacer on top of your door(s). Set your drawer front on top of the spacer—this will automatically set your gap. Reaching through the top of the cabinet, shoot a couple of small pin nails through the drawer box front into the back of your finished front while holding the drawer front in place with your other hand. This tacks the front in place and allows you to make minor adjustments before locking it into place with screws from the inside of the drawer box. Drill for pulls at this time, much the same as

THREE CABINET MODULES JOINED TOGETHER WITH SEX BOLTS

SEX BOLT

you would with face-frame cabinetry, since the cabinet is still on the bench. Again, a drilling template will speed up this effort.

You may decide that you want to attach a couple of boxes together on the bench before shipping. This makes the unit heavier, but it saves time in the field. We've found that joint connector bolts, often called sex bolts, work well for this. Clamp the boxes together and drill a 3/8-inch hole through both partitions at the same time; use at least six sex bolts per partition. Insert the hardware and tighten it up. The work will go much faster if you use a hex-head driver chucked up in your cordless. You may also wish to pre-drill for all the sex bolts before sending the cabinets out for installation. Again, this will save some time on the job, but it does take a little more effort in the shop. You'll need to either clamp all the adjacent boxes together before drilling, or carefully jig up the drilling on your partitions before assembly so that all the holes are in exactly the same location. Tack some small squares of plywood to the bottom of each box so that the deck is off the floor when you're sliding the boxes around. This helps prevent the edge-banding on the bottom deck from snag-

ging. Tack the blocks to the top of the upper cabinets since the bottoms are finished, and store them upside down while in the shop.

Pull your completed cabinet or cabinets off the bench and proceed to the next one. Be sure to label each unit as to where it is supposed to end up in the overall scheme. Use a corresponding labeling system on the drawings that will eventually be sent out to the site.

CHAPTER 7: APPENDICES

1. ALTERNATE ASSEMBLY TOOLS

There are a couple of readily available wood joinery tools that can be used as alternates in assembling cabinets and components. One is the plate joiner, sometimes referred to as a biscuit joiner. This handy tool is relatively inexpensive and can be used for a variety of applications— for face-frame assembly, door assembly, face-frame attachment to the case, etc. A small-diameter blade cuts a half-moon slot into two opposing pieces to be joined. A cross-grain wafer, or biscuit, which is made of compressed wood, is inserted in the slots with glue. The moisture in the glue swells the wafer and causes it to lock the joint fairly quickly. The two pieces being joined are usually placed in clamps for a short time to ensure that the joint is perfectly tight before the glue dries. Three sizes of biscuits are available for a variety of different applications.

Another tool that is being used more and more for joinery is the screw pocket machine. This machine comes in either a floor or bench model. Essentially, a router bit cuts a diagonal hole into one of the pieces of wood to be joined. The angle of the cut is precisely calculated so that when a screw is inserted into a hole that's automatically drilled at the bottom of the routed countersink, it pulls the opposing member tight. Again, this tool can be used for many of the same applications as listed above for the plate joiner. One disadvantage of this tool is that one side of the joint will have the pockets and screws exposed, whereas with a biscuit joiner the fastener is hidden.

TYPICAL POCKET-CUTTER APPLICATION SHOWING ATTACHMENT OF LIGHT RAIL ON A FRAMELESS UPPER CABEINT

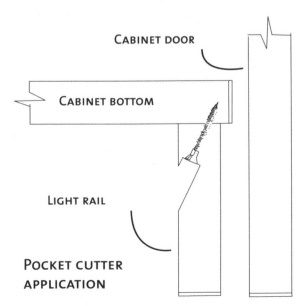

ALTERNATE METHOD USING NAILS AND GLUE

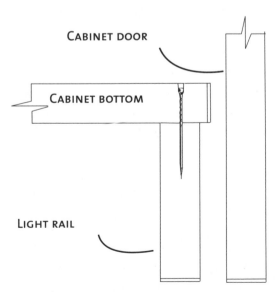

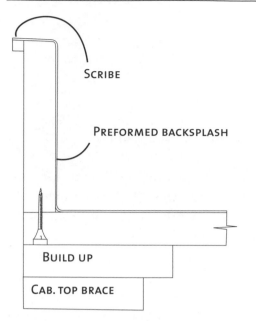

Scribe

Preformed backsplash

Build up

Cab. top brace

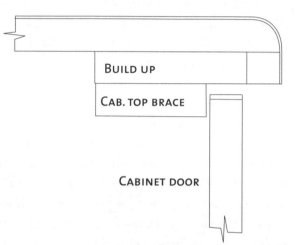

PREFORMED COUNTERTOP

Build up

Cab. top brace

Cabinet door

2. COUNTERTOP MATERIALS

Countertops are an important aspect of cabinet-making, but they are often delegated to specialists. Preformed plastic laminate tops, for example, require specialized machinery that is an impractical investment for the average cabinet shop. We'll discuss a number of countertop possibilities here and you can decide for yourself how much of this part of the project you wish to take on. But regardless of what you decide, you need to determine the thickness you wish to allow for the tops before you build the cabinets—typically we allow 1-1/2 inches. (Depending on the thickness of the finished countertop material, buildups can be used to make up the difference.) Take care not to exceed your standard heights. Most kitchen appliances are built to fit an overall height of 36 inches. Dishwashers require an opening under the countertop of 34-1/2 inches (thus the typical standard of a 1-1/2-inch allowance).

PLASTIC LAMINATE

Plastic laminate is one of the most popular countertop materials available. It's relatively inexpensive, easy to maintain, and available in literally hundreds of colors. Many of the names of the colors are interesting and creative—although you'd think that manufacturers would have run out of names by now, new ones just keep coming. Visit a home supply store to view color chips from a variety of manufacturers. Note that while many people use the word "Formica" to refer to all laminates, this isn't a trade name but a generic name.

Laminate comes in three grades for various applications. Vertical grade, which is 1/32 inch thick, is used primarily for vertical surfaces; its thinness makes the laminate easier to handle. Standard-grade laminate, which is 1/16 inch thick, is used for countertops—it's more durable than vertical grade. The third grade, post-form, is used almost exclusively by countertop manufacturers where contoured forming and bending are required.

If you or your clients want laminate counters,

SMART CLIPS   **WOOD-EDGE COUNTERTOP**

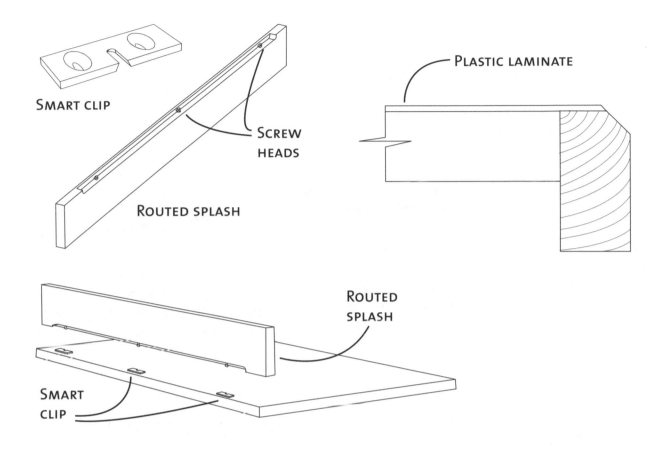

SMART CLIP

SCREW HEADS

ROUTED SPLASH

PLASTIC LAMINATE

ROUTED SPLASH

SMART CLIP

one option is to purchase pre-manufactured tops. They are generally made in blanks of 2-foot increments and come with a built-in drip edge, a preformed backsplash, and laminate end caps for finished ends. Note that these tops can be tricky to cut. It's even more challenging to cut miters on them because of that built-in splash. The color selection of pre-manufactured tops is limited, too, as only the popular colors are used for mass production. However, if you go to a custom countertop manufacturer, you will probably be able to get just about any color you desire. Be careful, though, as there may be a substantial lead time for exotic colors. You will need to build up these pre-manufactured tops by 3/4 inch, as they will most likely be produced at a thickness of 3/4 inch.

It's fairly straightforward to make your own laminate tops if you stay with square edges. Particleboard is a suitable substrate, although you may want to upgrade to MDO (medium density overlay) plywood if you are concerned about moisture around sinks and dishwashers and in other areas. Plywood doesn't swell if it gets wet the way particleboard does.

Use contact cement for bonding, but be sure to follow the directions on the label for application. A good trick is to lay your pre-glued laminate on top of the pre-glued substrate with 1/2-inch dowels spaced about 1 foot apart in between. Position the laminate exactly where you want it, then begin gluing at one end, removing the dowels one at a time until the pieces are joined. You have only one shot at this, since the glue grabs instantly. To ensure good adhesion, roll out every square inch with a laminate roller. Use tight joint fasteners at any field joint along with biscuits for alignment. These fasteners, sometimes referred to as draw bolts, are designed to pull and hold the two sections of countertop together. Inspect the joints carefully in the shop before sending the countertop out to the job—the laminate should be perfectly flush at the seams. Colored paste filler, which is made to fill seams, is available from laminate suppliers—it can disguise most small chips and imperfections.

Backsplashes can either be applied to the countertop before installation with screws from below, or attached after the countertop has been installed. The former will require an offset laminate trimmer, so you can get up close to the wall. After the top has been installed, laminate the top edges of the back and end splashes as well as the front edges of the end splashes while scribing to the wall at the same time. Then trim off the excess at the front of the splashes with your offset trimmer.

If you decide to mount your splashes after the top is in, "smart clips" are great devices to use. You install them with a measuring tool and driver that sets your screw at a predetermined depth so that the horseshoe-shaped plastic clip grabs the screw and pulls it tightly down to the countertop surface. Always use a bead of silicone (water-soluble for ease in cleaning up) under the backsplash in order to seal the joint.

Laminate tops are sometimes adorned with a wood edge. Attach this edge to the face of the countertop substrate with glue and nails, or if you prefer to avoid nails, simply glue and clamp. Sand the wood flush with the substrate. Lay the laminate over the entire top, including the wood edge, and trim with a chamfer router bit. The other option is to butt the wood edge to the face of the laminated substrate, making sure that you've aligned the two top surfaces perfectly. Clamps and a generous amount of glue should be used with this type of joint to ensure that no voids remain where moisture can penetrate.

TILE TOPS

Along with plastic laminate, ceramic tile is a pretty and functional counter material. Again, there are literally hundreds of colors and patterns to choose from. But tile-setting is a specialty, and unless you're really versatile, it's better to leave this job to a professional. Typically, cabinetmakers supply the plywood substrate. Never use particleboard, since it swells when it comes in contact with water. Because there is usually an allowance of 1-1/2 inches for the countertop, the 3/4-inch substrate still gives the tile-setter 3/4 inch to work with, which is generally sufficient. If the tile will be set in mortar, it's possible to exceed an overall cabinet height of 36 inches, or if the tile is thinset, using only tile adhesive, the overall height may be a little less. You should always communicate with the tile setter to learn the exact requirements, and then provide the appropriate substrate. Be sure to get this in your bid, as it all adds up in the end.

SOLID-SURFACE MATERIALS

Solid-surface countertops such as Corian and Avenite to name just two, are gaining in popularity, although they are expensive. A wide variety of beautiful colors and patterns has been developed in recent years, and many homeowners have been attracted to this relatively new product. Solid-surface tops require special techniques to manufacture and are often out of the realm of most cabinet shops. The suppliers of the material will not even sell to you unless you've taken a fabrication and installation course, which is generally a day's worth of instruction at your shop, after which they will certify you for using their products. Many shops specialize in solid-surface countertops, and you might be well advised to hire one of them. Warranties can be a big issue with these products, and you will want to avoid potential problems down the road.

OTHER COUNTERTOP MATERIALS

Solid maple butcher blocks are sometimes used as countertops, and they can be attractive and functional. But don't try to make these in your shop unless you have nothing but time and a lot of wood—blanks can readily be purchased in 2-foot increments. The blanks come with a factory sealer, which we always sand off. In rounding over the edges, which are sometimes sharper than is desirable, you tend to compromise the finish that's already there. Also, the sealer isn't particularly attractive. (Don't take the factory finish off the bottom of the blank, however, as that keeps the top stable.) To coat the blank, we apply two or three coats of mineral oil, which produce a soft, hand-rubbed look. Don't use a petroleum-based finish on butcher block, since it will contaminate any food that's prepared on it. Vegetable oil is also not a suitable finish, because over time it becomes rancid.

Other possibilities for countertops, which tend to be reserved for the well to do, are granite and marble. Again, these tops must be provided by people who work with this material on a regular basis. Soapstone is becoming popular now, and we've even seen poured concrete used for countertops. There's no end to the variety. As a cabinetmaker, you may want to stay away from countertops altogether and subcontract this work. There's a good argument for sticking to what you do best and hiring those who do what they do best. Your risk is limited and your costs are fixed. There's nothing wrong with including this part of the job in your contract, subbing it out, and then marking it up for your coordination time—it's a good way to make extra money on a project. But as usual, make sure that clients always know exactly what they're getting.

3. A SLIDE-OUT BREADBOARD

Manufactured breadboards are readily available from cabinetmakers' supply houses.

TO INSTALL

Using a saber saw, cut a slot in the top rail of the face frame directly over a bay. File it smooth. Fasten two grooved tracks to the cabinet walls directly behind the slot. Adjust the action of the breadboard by shimming or planing the tracks in the same manner that the support blocks for the drawer slide hardware are adjusted (page 64).

BREADBOARD

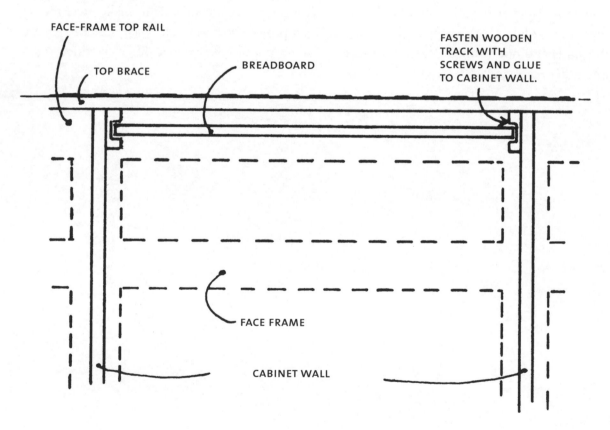

FACE-FRAME TOP RAIL

TOP BRACE

BREADBOARD

FASTEN WOODEN TRACK WITH SCREWS AND GLUE TO CABINET WALL.

FACE FRAME

CABINET WALL

4. FINISHING A BASE (TOE-KICK)

For a finished toe-kick, apply 1/4-inch fine plywood over the base after installation. If necessary, scribe the "skin" to the finished floor.

FINISHED CORNER DETAIL

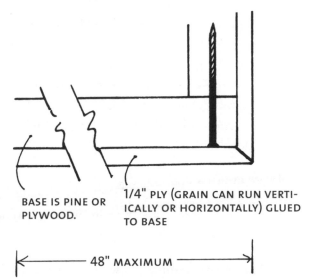

BASE IS PINE OR PLYWOOD.

1/4" PLY (GRAIN CAN RUN VERTICALLY OR HORIZONTALLY) GLUED TO BASE

|←——— 48" MAXIMUM ———→|

CLOSING AN OPEN MITER

If the miter is slightly open, it can be filled with glue and burnished shut with a nail set, then sanded when dry.

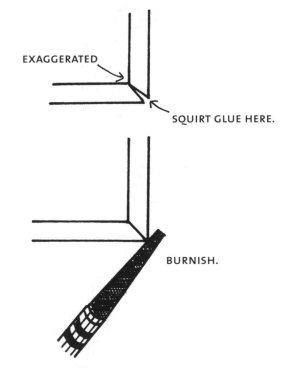

EXAGGERATED

SQUIRT GLUE HERE.

BURNISH.

5. Lazy Susans

The corner cabinet that holds the rotating shelves is laid out full size on a one-piece deck. Because of the bulk of this cabinet, be sure to leave the toe-kick off or you may not be able to get the cabinet into the house. If turned on its back, the 31-1/4-inch unit will fit through a 32-inch doorway.

There are two main configurations:

1. The shelf unit alone turns inside the cabinet. The doors are hinged on the face frame.

2. The shelves and outside doors turn as one unit. While this configuration is usually pre-ferred by customers, the construction process is quite involved and requires precision.

Deck layout

1. Cut the deck.

2. Draw a dotted line from the inside corner to the back corner.

3. Mark the center on the dotted line.

4. Using a beam compass, obtain the largest possible circle that will clear at least 1-1/2 inches all around. Note that the diameter of the plywood shelf is 1/4 inch less because of the 1/8-inch band.

TYPES OF LAZY SUSANS

1 INDEPENDENT SHELVES
TOP VIEW WITHOUT TOP BRACES

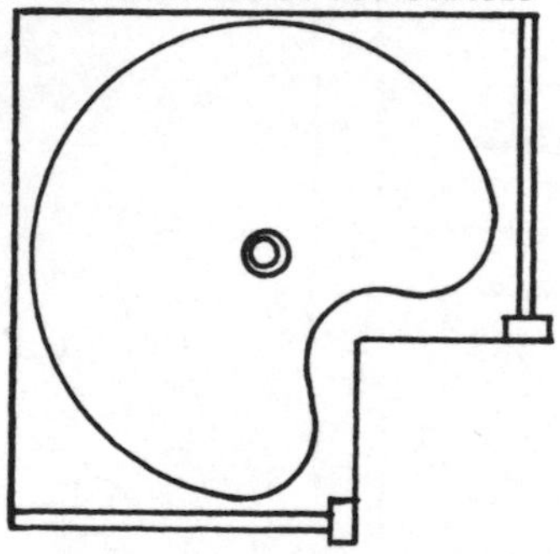

METAL SHELVES, PIVOTS, AND POLE ARE COMMERCIALLY AVAILABLE.

TWO DOORS HINGED ON FACE FRAME

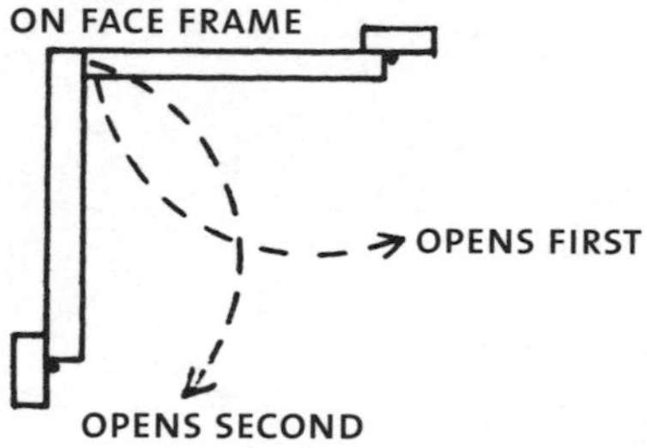

OPENS FIRST

OPENS SECOND

BIFOLD DOORS HINGED ON ONE SIDE

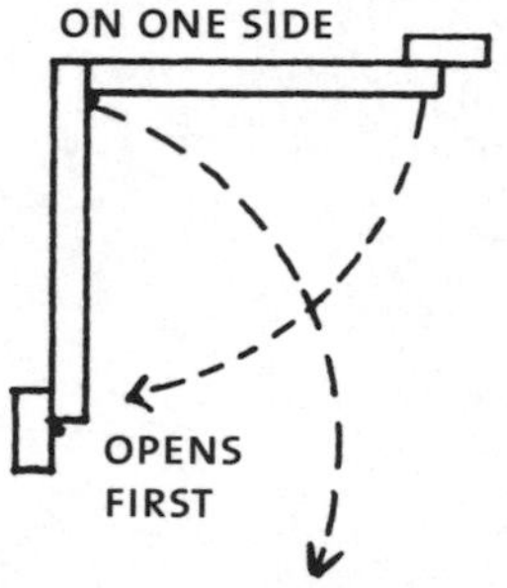

OPENS FIRST

OPENS SECOND

2 SHELVES AND DOOR MOVE TOGETHER

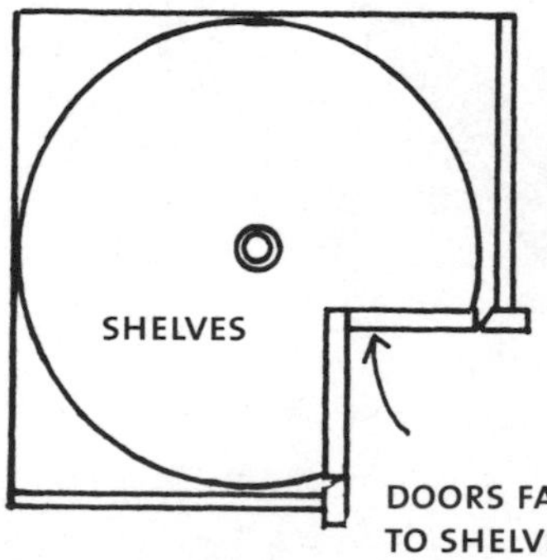

SHELVES

SHELVES ARE 3/4" PLY BANDED WITH 1/8" X 1-1/2" SOLID LUMBER OR PLY, USED WITH METAL PIVOTS AND POLE.

← USE SPLIT-STILE HERE IF NECESSARY (SEE APPENDIX 6).

DOORS FASTENED TO SHELVES

LAYOUT MEASUREMENTS

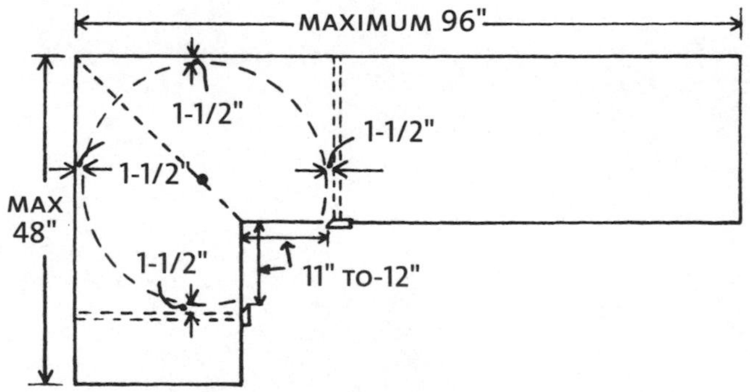

MAXIMUM 96"

MAX 48"

1-1/2"

1-1/2"

1-1/2"

1-1/2"

11" TO-12"

BUILDING THE SHELVES

You can purchase pre-made metal or plastic shelves from cabinetmaking-supply stores. If you want to make your own, here's a method. Use an overarm style of saw guard and don't lose control of this operation because the results could be disastrous.

Usually there are two shelves.

1. Cut 3/4-inch plywood squares for the shelves.

2. Cut a notch for the doors on the table saw.

3. Cut the circle as shown below.

4. Set a pivot at R (the radius of a 3/4-inch plywood shelf).

5. Place the shelf on the pivot in the position shown in the top view. Start the saw with the blade completely retracted.

6. Hang on to the deck firmly and slowly raise the blade of the table saw so that it will make a 1/8-inch cut in the underside of the shelf.

7. Rotate the shelf blank one full turn.

8. Raise the blade 1/8 inch.

9. Repeat procedures #7 and #8 until the circle is fully cut.

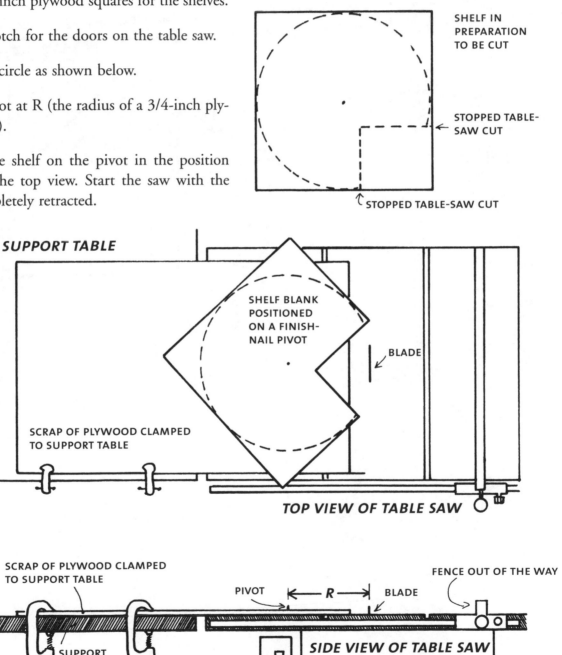

SHELF IN PREPARATION TO BE CUT

STOPPED TABLE-SAW CUT

STOPPED TABLE-SAW CUT

SUPPORT TABLE

SHELF BLANK POSITIONED ON A FINISH-NAIL PIVOT

BLADE

SCRAP OF PLYWOOD CLAMPED TO SUPPORT TABLE

TOP VIEW OF TABLE SAW

SCRAP OF PLYWOOD CLAMPED TO SUPPORT TABLE

FENCE OUT OF THE WAY

PIVOT

R

BLADE

SUPPORT TABLE

SIDE VIEW OF TABLE SAW

BANDING THE SHELVES

Cut a strip of lumber or 1/8-inch plywood to 1/8 inch by 1-1/2 inch by the circumference plus a bit. Birch works well. Glue, nail, and clamp the banding to the shelf

BUILDING THE CABINET

Construct the cabinet according to the procedures already discussed with the following exceptions. Leave off the 1/4-inch plywood back to insert the shelf unit. Build the top braces and install them in the order shown. Do not attach the base

SHELF BANDING

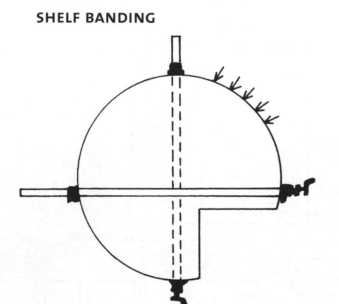

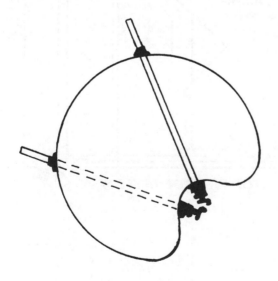

CABINET CONSTRUCTION

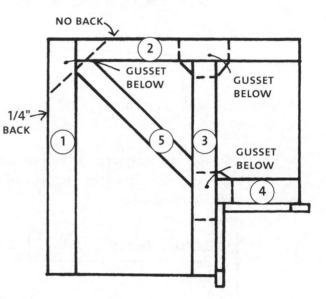

BUILDING THE SHELF UNIT

Drill the shelves accurately for the pole. Then cut the spacers. Construct as shown.

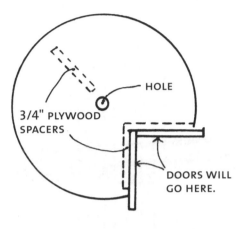

3/4" PLYWOOD SPACERS

HOLE

DOORS WILL GO HERE.

NAIL AND GLUE TO SECURE SPACERS.

TWO TEMPORARY SCREWS WILL HOLD DOORS UNTIL ADJUSTMENT IS COMPLETE.

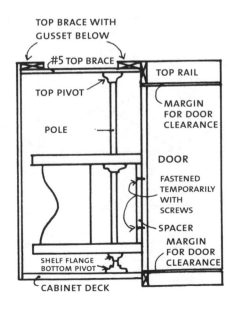

TOP BRACE WITH GUSSET BELOW

#5 TOP BRACE

TOP PIVOT

POLE

TOP RAIL

MARGIN FOR DOOR CLEARANCE

DOOR

FASTENED TEMPORARILY WITH SCREWS

SPACER

MARGIN FOR DOOR CLEARANCE

SHELF FLANGE BOTTOM PIVOT

CABINET DECK

FASTENING THE DOORS TO THE SHELF UNIT AND INSTALLING THE SHELF/DOOR UNIT IN THE CABINET

1. Locate the bottom pivot on the dotted diagonal line on the deck as close as possible to its predetermined place. Attach with one screw to allow adjustment.

2. Mount the top pivot in the same manner on the #5 top brace. The #5 brace can be temporarily placed under the other top braces.

3. Cut the pole to length so 1/4 inch remains in the upper pivot.

4. Slip the pole into place with the hardware already attached to the shelf bottoms. Tighten the flange to position the unit on the pole.

5. Slide the unit through the open back in the cabinet.

6. Adjust the bottom pivot until the doors align with the bottom and side edges.

7. Adjust the #5 top brace similarly.

8. Check the gap between the face frame and the door assembly. It should be approximately 1/8 inch. If the gap is too tight or uneven, sand the edges of the doors accordingly to produce a consistent margin.

9. Gently swing the unit through one full rotation to check clearances.

10. Secure the pivots, #5 top brace, and doors to the shelf unit.

11. Install a bullet catch or similar locking mechanism to align the door with the face frame when the doors are in the closed position.

6. MAKING A SPLIT STILE

The obvious places to divide cabinets are at ends, appliances, and corners. But occasionally this will not be possible, as illustrated in the diagram.

1. Make a 2-1/8-inch wide stile.

2. Drill a pilot hole, clearance, and countersink holes as indicated by the arrows.

3. Rip the stile exactly in half and screw it back together.

4. Referring to the section detail, build two cases, allowing for 1/4 inch between them.

5. Mark, bore, and assemble the face frame as one unit. Bore shortened holes in the split stile.

6. Position the cabinets on their backs and fasten through the partitions in front and back with 1/4-inch plywood blocking.

7. Attach the joined face frame to the joined cabinets.

8. Treating the units as one, clean up, sand, hang the drawers and doors, and then separate for delivery.

SPLIT-STILE CONSTRUCTION

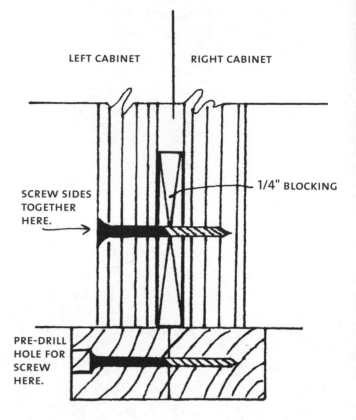

LEFT CABINET   RIGHT CABINET

1/4" BLOCKING

SCREW SIDES TOGETHER HERE.

PRE-DRILL HOLE FOR SCREW HERE.

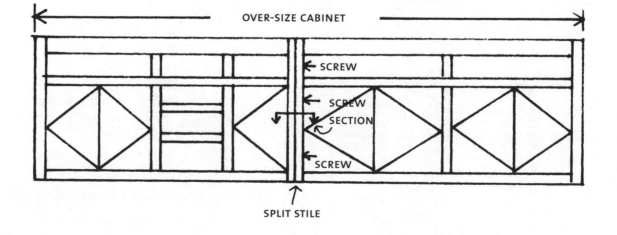

OVER-SIZE CABINET

SCREW

SCREW

SECTION

SCREW

SPLIT STILE

7. WALL-TO-WALL FACE-FRAME INSTALLATION

Many times a cabinet must fit in an alcove or between two walls. There are two simple methods to deal with this—trim-strip and loose stile.

TRIM-STRIP

Make a cabinet with two wall ends 1/2 inch less than the distance between the walls. When installed, the cabinet slides into place and a trim strip is nailed over the gap.

LOOSE STILE

The loose stile uses no trim. A cabinet with two wall ends is fit exactly into the opening by leaving one of the face-frame stiles loose.

1. Lay out and bore the face frame as usual.

2. Assemble with the loose stile in place but do not glue it.

3. Glue the face frame to the cabinet in the normal position and sand—but keep the stile free.

4. Bevel the outside edge of the stile and shorten the dowel as shown. Glue the dowel in the loose stile.

5. When installing, remove the stile and slide the cabinet into place.

6. Scribe the fixed stile to fit exactly.

7. Test the place of the loose stile. Sand as necessary to obtain a tight pressed fit.

8. Glue the stile in place and hand-sand the surface.

FACE FRAME-FRONT VIEW

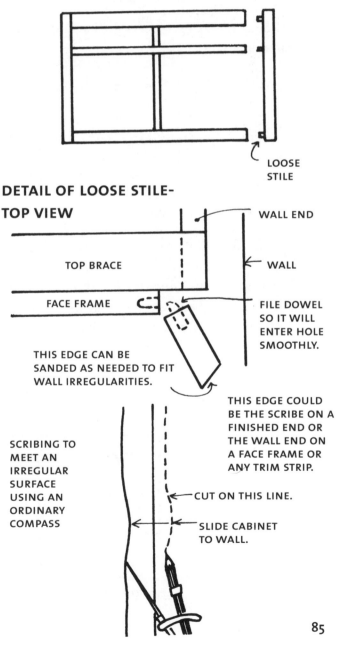

LOOSE STILE

DETAIL OF LOOSE STILE-TOP VIEW

WALL END

TOP BRACE

WALL

FACE FRAME

FILE DOWEL SO IT WILL ENTER HOLE SMOOTHLY.

THIS EDGE CAN BE SANDED AS NEEDED TO FIT WALL IRREGULARITIES.

THIS EDGE COULD BE THE SCRIBE ON A FINISHED END OR THE WALL END ON A FACE FRAME OR ANY TRIM STRIP.

SCRIBING TO MEET AN IRREGULAR SURFACE USING AN ORDINARY COMPASS

CUT ON THIS LINE.

SLIDE CABINET TO WALL.

USING A TRIM STRIP-TOP VIEW

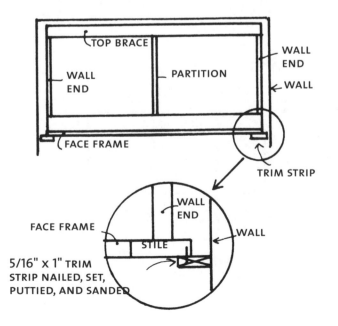

TOP BRACE

WALL END

WALL

PARTITION

WALL

WALL END

FACE FRAME

TRIM STRIP

WALL END

FACE FRAME

WALL

STILE

5/16" x 1" TRIM STRIP NAILED, SET, PUTTIED, AND SANDED

8. FALSE DRAWER FRONT

When there is a sink or cooktop or other obstruction in a drawer space, a false front to match the drawers is usually installed.

1. Cut two or three scraps of 1/4-inch plywood to 2-1/2 inches by 6 inches.

2. Put a screw through the center of each.

3. Position the scraps on the back of the front, as shown.

4. Place the front over the face-frame opening.

5. Rotate the scraps so as to grab behind the face frame.

6. Tighten the screws until the plywood bows a bit.

7. Adjust the false front to align it with the previously hung drawers and doors.

8. Tack the plywood top and bottom to the face frame with brads or staples.

In frameless cabinets, merely add a 3/4-inch thick filler about 1/2 inch narrower than the false front (so the filler doesn't show below the false front), in between the cabinet sides. Fasten the front to the cabinet by screwing through this filler and into the false front.

INSTALLING A FALSE FRONT

TOP BRACE

COUNTERTOP

TOP FACE-FRAME RAIL

PROPOSED SINK

FRONT TO MATCH OTHER DOORS

1/4" SCRAP PLYWOOD

MIDDLE FACE FRAME

VIEW FROM INSIDE CABINET AT STEP #4

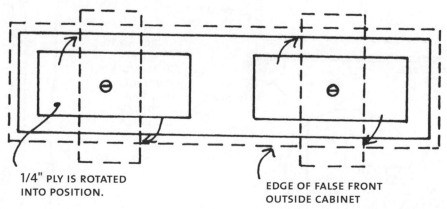

1/4" PLY IS ROTATED INTO POSITION.

EDGE OF FALSE FRONT OUTSIDE CABINET

9. Floor-to-ceiling cabinets

The height and depth of floor-to-ceiling cabinets require special attention. In order to stand up such a tall box in a standard 96-inch room, the base unit must be left loose to be attached on the site. Since the upright cabinet is 1/2 inch short of the ceiling, its top rail must be 1/2 inch narrower than adjacent uppers so that the doors will line up visually along the ceiling. The cabinet is also a little bit deeper (24-3/4 inch) than the adjacent lower cabinets. This provides for a clean intersection of the countertop and the side of the oven cabinet.

SHOP-MADE STOP

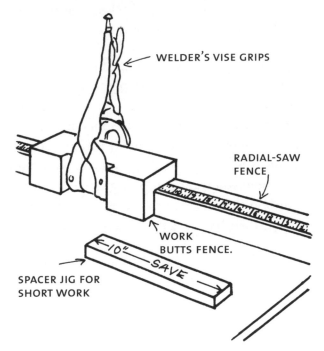

WELDER'S VISE GRIPS

RADIAL-SAW FENCE

WORK BUTTS FENCE.

SPACER JIG FOR SHORT WORK

←10"→ SAVE

10. Measuring tips

A few measuring tips to save time when cutting:

There are some nice, well-calibrated stops on the market for use with radial saws. It's very easy to make your own, however, as shown. Carefully attach a tape to the back fence, adjusted perfectly so that it indicates the exact distance from the blade. Using a pair of welder's vise grips as a quick-release clamp, build the device illustrated. Yes, it rules out the mitering function of the saw unless the first 15 inches of tape are eliminated. But bear in mind that in a commercial situation, it is economical to use the radial saw only for 90° crosscutting, relying on an electric miter saw and the table saw for miters.

Your table saw will obviously come with a fence. Unless it's really accurate and quick to operate, consider investing in a high-quality fence. This might be one of your best investments, since you will be spending so much time at the saw. A good fence will save you many hours of trying to get those precision cuts just right.

Always set up your cabinets after completion, preferably in the order in which they will be installed. Measure everything at this point to be sure that no mistakes were made. It will make you sick when you discover an error in your shop, but you would be even sicker if you discovered the error on the job and your client's important dinner party was less than a week away. It's a good idea to make installation notes on the cabinets themselves—this makes it easier for the installer, especially if the installer is someone other than you. If pieces are to be joined together in the field, be sure this is done in the shop as well. Use tick-marks after pre-assembly to ensure that everything goes back together in exactly the same way.

11. SOME THOUGHTS ON ADVERTISING AND MARKETING

Attracting customers is an ongoing concern. Consider these important advertising factors: quality work, word of mouth, and personal calls to potential buyers. These potential buyers include builders and decorators, who you can track down through the yellow pages of local phone books. Another way to "spread the word" is with publicity—look for opportunities to promote your work in free newspaper feature articles. You can also take out paid advertisements in the yellow pages and other publications. Business cards are a must. Always photograph your work both in the shop and at the final installation. Carry prints with you all the time. Don't overlook the value of a well-located shop. The extra rent can be seen as an advertising expense.

Don't ever let your guard down when it comes to marketing. It's far better to have too much work than too little or none at all. Spend a given amount of time each week tracking leads, talking to people, looking for that next job. The more contacts you have, the more likely you will have ongoing work. Remember that referrals are your best source of new work, and, in that light, keeping the customer happy becomes paramount.

12. THE DYNAMICS OF EMPLOYEES

Once you reach a certain size, you will soon realize that you can't do everything yourself. Here's the problem that every small business owner faces. The reason you started a business, or plan to start a business, is probably that you're very good at what you do. The challenge now is that you will have to find someone else who is as good as you are to take your place, since you'll be moving more and more into management. You'll find out soon enough that no one else will be able to do the job as well as you can or exactly the way you want it done, so you may as well get used to it. It really doesn't matter though, because the job will get done and since you've freed yourself up to do more important things, even more will get done in a shorter amount of time.

You probably won't find woodworking graduates fresh out of school willing to ply their new trade, since there are very few these days. This means that you'll be locating and training individuals who are motivated and interested in cabinetmaking. Once you hire employees, be very clear about how you want something done by actually showing them what to do. Explain things as you go, then have them try the operation while you watch. Tell them how long the operation or series of operations should take. Once they have the hang of it, let them go at it. If you've done your job correctly, you'll be surprised at how well things turn out. Motivated and interested people want to do a good job and all they need is some guidance, encouragement, and praise for a job well done.

A sense of teamwork is critical for the success of any business, and you can help instill this by including employees in the decision-making process as much as possible. Also, let employees know that you truly care about their welfare. Set the tone by never asking an employee to do something that you wouldn't do yourself: Above all else, be sensitive to your employees' needs and at the first sign of any discontent, address the issue or issues with those involved firmly, aggressively, and respectfully. By maintaining clear and open lines of communication, you will develop long-term, loyal relationships that will mutually benefit everyone involved.

13. SHOP REQUIREMENTS

There are many books, magazines, journals, and, of course, the Internet, where tools, materials, supplies, and ideas are discussed. Aside from referring to these sources, visit other cabinet shops and make a point of getting to know other cabinetmakers. For the most part, they'll be willing to share their knowledge. Find out what they're doing and how they're doing it, how they've arranged their shops, etc. This exchange of ideas can be mutually beneficial and often results in long-term friendships.

This list includes only the basics. As you grow and expand, always seek to improve your working environment by reinvesting in tools, equipment, and other things that will make your shop a safe and comfortable place to work.

Your shop should include:

- adequate square footage for your needs (remember, assembled cabinets are mostly air and take up lots of space).

- adequate electrical service.

- a level assembly area.

- good lighting and ventilation.

- a heat source if you work in a colder climate (60° is the minimum temperature for glue drying).

- space for the table saw and radial saw to be placed adjacent to each other, since they are often used alternately during cutting.

FIXTURES AND ACCESSORIES

The following fixtures and accessories will make your work go faster and more easily:

• an 18-inch high assembly table. Make the top from two or three 4-foot by 8-foot particleboard sheets, replacing the top one as needed. Keep the upper sheet waxed to prevent glue drops from sticking.

• a couple of different heights of sawhorses

• a workbench with a woodworker's vise

• storage racks and shelves for tools and hardware

• a small tool dolly or mobile toolbox

• storage racks for plywood and lumber near the table saw

• a support table surrounding the table saw. It should allow the cutting of sheet materials in any direction without offcuts falling off.

• a support table for the radial saw. It should extend at least 12 feet to one side of the blade and have a calibrated adjustable stop for cutting to length (page 87). The top is waxed particleboard. A motorized chop saw can also be set into this bench and aligned with the fence.

• clamps—you can't ever have too many clamps, but here are some suggestions:

• 6 to 10 spring clamps—like large clothespins with rubber jaws

• 10 deep-throated adjustable c-clamps with a 3/8-inch by 1-1/2-inch by 18-inch bar

• 3/4-inch pipe clamps: three 12-footers, three 8-footers, and twenty 5-footers

• C-clamps, cast or adjustable: ten 6-inch clamps and ten 3-inch clamps

• two 18-inch by 24-inch dollies with four swivel casters as close to the floor as possible for moving large cabinets

• one or more table-height dollies (18 inches by 24 inches) for wheeling around small bundles of material

• one large material dolly for stacking case parts before moving them to the assembly area

• carpet remnants to protect finished surfaces

BENCH TOOLS

Here are the essentials:

• a 10-inch table saw with a 48- to 60-tooth carbide-tipped combination blade

• a 10-inch or 12-inch radial saw with a 48- to 60-tooth carbide-tipped crosscutting blade

• air stapler (5/8 inch to 1-1/2 inch capacity)

• an air nailer (1 inch to 1-1/2 inch capacity)

• horizontal boring machine with carbide bit

• a drill press

For frameless cabinetry you will want:

• a line-boring machine and edge-bander

Other highly recommended tools and equipment include:

• a router table (the "poor man's shaper")

• a shaper

• an edge-sander

• dust collection equipment

PORTABLE POWER TOOLS

Many portable power tools (sanders, routers, drills), are made in air-driven models for heavy industrial use. They are lighter, more durable, and have fewer moving parts. They are also expensive, require a large volume of air, and are limited to shop use.

- belt sander(s)

- 3/8-inch variable-speed reversible drill(s)

- router(s): 1hp, 1/4-inch collet minimum. Check handles, switch, weight, collet ejection, ease of adjustment, and noise before you buy. Use carbide bits.

- a biscuit joiner

- a bench grinder for sharpening

- 4-1/2-inch by 4-inch block sander(s)

- 4-1/2-inch by 9-inch vibrating sander(s)

- 7-1/4-inch circular saw

- a 3-inch power planer

- a saber saw

HAND TOOLS

Hand tools are the life blood of a serious cabinetmaker. Most of us take great pride in our tools and treat them with great respect. High-quality tools are an extension of your hands, and, if treated properly, will give you a lifetime of service and satisfaction. Keep your tools sharp and clean, and use them only for their intended purpose. For example, you would never use your fine wood chisels for opening putty cans!

Many cumulative hours can be saved by keeping the following tools in your shop apron or pouch while you're working.

- a pencil

- a 16-foot tape measure

- a combination square

- a 16-oz. hammer

- a nail set(s)

- a follow-through nail punch

- fa our-in-one screwdriver

- a 3/4-inch chisel

- a nail-grabber pliers

- a putty knife

- a cabinet scraper

Keep the following tools nearby on a rack or dolly:

- a dowelling jig

- a full set of chisels

- an assortment of files and wood rasps

- a carpenter's square

- a sheetrock square

- hand saws

- a straight edge (36 inches minimum)

- a large adjustable angle gauge

- a beam compass

- vise grips

MISCELLANEOUS TOOL TIPS

• Blow dust out of housings and bearings often, using an air compressor and nozzle.

• To avoid down-time, keep duplicate bits, blades, and tools on hand whenever possible.

• Find a good tool-repair shop. Don't hesitate to call many hundreds of miles for good professional service. Shipping companies often provides a service that is less trouble than driving to a local shop. Manufacturers' warranties are not much good if another tool has to be bought while the broken one is away being repaired for ten weeks.

• Never leave power tools perched in precarious positions. Always set them on the floor during intermittent use to avoid tripping over the power cord and dragging them onto the floor. Getting into this habit can save you hundreds of dollars per year on repairs.

• Maintain a maintenance schedule, regularly inspecting belts, blades, and brushes, and lubricating where necessary.

• Sharp tools are essential. This goes for sawblades, router bits, planer blades, chisels, shapers, and anything else you can think of that cuts wood. It's not only more pleasurable to work with sharp tools, it's safer.

14. MATERIALS AND SUPPLIES

A wide range of materials suitable for cabinetmaking exists—from particleboard to fine veneers. Economy-grade cabinets might consist of particleboard interiors, while premium-grade cabinets may have prefinished birch or maple interiors. The budget of each cabinet job will dictate what materials are used, but most people pick a standard product and stick with it for most of their jobs. Not only is it expensive to stock a large variety of materials, it also takes up valuable space. Birch plywood is commonly used for interiors as is melamine, for those who want a durable, washable surface. Drawer boxes are often made from melamine, 9-ply birch, or solid lumber.

Cabinet fronts are generally made with hardwood, although knotty pine or fir is popular for a more rustic look. Try to avoid tropical forest hardwoods unless they are certified as sustainable. Many species of wood are becoming increasingly expensive as demand continues, and certain types of high-quality lumber can sometimes be hard to find.

Find a lumber and plywood dealer who you can trust and build a rapport with. Try to develop a long-term relationship with your suppliers. If you're a loyal customer, your suppliers will bend over backward to help you out if you get into a bind. Stay closely in touch with prices and always be aware of what you are being charged.

You will need a good stash of supplies on hand and you will need to replenish them fairly regularly. These are things like glue, sandpaper, masking tape, wood putty, dowels, biscuits, wood screws, nails, shelf pins, dust masks, etc. Keep a list of items that you use, and watch your inventory level. It's very frustrating to stop what you're doing to run down to the hardware store for a bottle of glue or some such silly thing. Generally these are considered overhead items, and are not necessarily charged against an individual job. Again, find a cabinet wholesaler who specializes in cabinetmaking supplies and equipment. If you're in or near a major city, suppliers will often make deliveries to your door each week. Purchase as much as you can in bulk. It's always cheaper, and it saves you time by not having to deal with replenishing your supplies as often.

15. LAST WORDS

The key to success in business is largely a matter of how you manage your affairs and the attitude with which you do so. It's not hard. Treat your clients and your employees as if only they mattered. Respond promptly to their wishes and concerns, and communicate as effectively as you can throughout your relationships with them. Be firm and decisive when necessary—your options are many, but yet your time is limited. Maintain organization in your office, your shop, and your daily life. Approach every workday with honesty, integrity, and a winning attitude. Remember that achieving the impossible takes only a little longer.

For every page in this book, there are many exceptions and variations to choose from. There will always be questions and uncertainty, but that's just the way it is. Don't be afraid to be creative and to try something if you think there's a chance that it will work. When you're an old-timer, you'll be able to look back at all the dumb mistakes you made and smile. Yet at the same time you will have the satisfaction of knowing that you were engaged in one of the greatest careers there is—the art of cabinetmaking.

INDEX

PUBLISHER	JOHN KELSEY
EDITOR	LAURA TRINGALI
ILLUSTRATOR	GINA ROMAN
SCANNING	BRAN CHAPMAN
PAGE LAYOUT	MORGAN KELSEY
COVER DESIGN	PEGGY BLOOMER
MANUFACTURING	SHERIDAN PRESS